What people are saying about Curtis A.
the Doctor… So Fix the Pi

Curtis Cowan's "You're The Doctor…So Fix The Problem!" Is the ultimate game plan for assuring the highest quality of customer service in any organization. With this well written, engaging, interactive book, I can access Cowan's experientially-based, professional technology every day. I feel as if I have a ready-made coach at hand supporting and prompting me to reach for the highest level of excellence thus, making a lasting positive first impression on every single customer by doing it right the first time every time."
--Dr. Alice Coner-Edwards,
Author "Families in Crisis"
In-house Marketing Coordinator
Cendant Corporation-Fairfield Resorts

This is a breakthrough book, with new and important ideas for how to get and keep customers in your place of business. After reading it, you will be a believer…that getting and keeping customers threw treating customers as the Doctor, really brings in a clear picture of what you should be doing to keep the customers happy, it showed me something new and improved my sales. And I'm sure it will do the same for you.
--Nelson Pugh ("Uncle Fatty")
Salesman,
Jim McKay Chevrolet

"Curtis Cowan's "You're The Doctor…So Fix The Problem" is a first-rate resource for understanding the rules of customer interface. This book is a customer focused, educational and motivational commerce tool that can be used by small entrepreneurs, midsize businesses and large corporations. The essence of the message is you never get a second chance to make a first impression."
--Louise Williams Bishop
State Representative
192nd Legislative District

Until reading Curtis Cowan's "You're The Doctor…So Fix The Problem" I thought I had seen it all, particularly after my own work in providing service for 50 years in the U.S. Army, Dept. Of Commerce and Residential Real Estate Sales. His analogy of the Doctor is new, refreshing and completely apt in an examination of how to provide successful service. Readers of this book can instantly relate to personal experience (I know I did) and apply Mr. Cowan's ideas to literally every kind of business venture."
--Colonel Ronald T. Cyr
U.S. Army, (Retired)

YOU'RE THE DOCTOR...
SO FIX THE PROBLEM!

**A FRESH APPROACH TO *EXCELLENT*
CUSTOMER SERVICE**

By

Curtis A. Cowan

Published by

The
Cowan C. Kean
Group
Publishing House

Silver Spring

ISBN: 978-0-9790759-0-2

Dedication

I have been blessed many times over, with so many wonderful people and to all of you, I say thank you. But as I sit here thinking about the whole process of writing this book, the most important fact is that my **Higher Power** has seen me threw this all and that both of my parents are still alive to see the finish results, and this is the best blessing any person could ask for. This book is dedicated to my family: Mom and Dad (*Rosa lee Cowan, Frank W. Cowan II*) I love you both, thank you. My son *Taylor Lee Curtis Cowan*, live to be your best always, I will always be with you in life and death. *Kean Lim*, my love, who has stuck with me through the deepest and hardest of times and still remains true—I love you! *Renetta and Arthur Poland-Cowan, Frank Cowan III, and Jennifer Chung and family.*

Author's Acknowledgments

Thanks to *Gary Anderson* an extraordinary editor and writer, for his contributions to this book project, and who has been a true friend throughout this project (www.iowa.com). And most importantly, thanks to *Robert Moment* the person who inspired and guided me through this whole project. Without you, Robert, this book would never have come to life. Thanks (www.sellintegrity.com).

Table of Contents

Introduction

With the number of consumers seeking top-quality customer service at an all-time high, there has never been a better time to start looking for ways to attract those customers, and to keep them coming back. Accomplishing both of those goals involves just one simple concept: providing superior customer service. Implement a program of extraordinary customer service, and your business will grow—guaranteed!

Customers will walk away from every transaction satisfied, and they'll keep coming back, again and again. What's more, they will tell their friends and associates, and those people can also become lifetime customers to your place of business. Everyone wins, and your business will continue to increase in both sales and number of customers.

In this book, you'll be reading, step-by-step, how you and your employees can ensure that every one of your customers are treated fairly and honestly, always with the goal of turning them into the best kind of customers—repeat customers. This book is designed to help ambitious companies improve and rise above their competitors by focusing all their efforts on proving great customer service, all day, every day.

It doesn't matter which rung of the corporate ladder you're on—CEO, manager, supervisor, salesperson, phone sales, stock room, mail handler—the key to your company's success, and your own, can be summed up in just three simple words: great customer service.

How the Concept Started

I've been in the business of customer service for more than twenty years, and I've worked at nearly every rung of that corporate ladder, which has given me a true understanding of what great customer service means—for both customers and companies. I've been a cook at McDonald's, worked in construction, and with time I gradually transitioned into more white-collar positions as a supervisor, a manager, a district manager, and now am the owner of my own company. Over the last two decades I've learned many secrets for getting—and then keeping—customers. All those secrets have one thing in common: the resolving of all customer service issues fairly, honestly, and promptly.

I've been on both sides of the counter, as a customer and as an employee, and what you'll be learning in this book are the keys to what I've seen and learned about providing great customer service. I've always had a passion for seeing people being treated right, and I've also believed that everyone has it in them to achieve greater things and to make life better for everyone with whom they come in contact—whether it's their friends, family, community, or the customers they meet daily at their place of business Over the years, I came to realize that I may not be able to change the world as a whole, but I could take care of my little corner, one person, and one issue at a time, making sure that every interaction I entered into was a win/win for everyone concerned. I treated everyone as fairly as I possibly could, and I discovered that, in almost every situation, the person I was dealing with responded in kind.

That became the concept upon which I've based my success. I try to make a difference in the life of one person at a time—and it has worked well for me for more than two decades in the business world.

Over the years, I began to realize that the one place I always saw as having a high rate of success with customer service was at the doctor's office. I've interviewed thousands of customers over the years, and I discovered that I wasn't alone in that observation. I found that more than 90% of the customers I interviewed about their visits to the doctor's office said that they had been happy with the way they were treated and with the results of their visit.

Think about your last visit to the doctor. Everyone involved, from the moment you walked in the door to the moment you were finished, they did everything in their power to make your visit as pleasant and satisfying as possible. They were totally focused on your needs, on your concerns, and on finding a solution to the situation that brought you into the office that day. There was never a doubt in your mind that their sole concern was for your welfare and satisfaction.

Armed with that knowledge, I have employed that same concept to my business dealings throughout my career. I treated every customer I've come into contact with as if I'm their doctor, and regardless of their needs, I went out of my way to make sure those needs were met. When my customers walked away, they knew that I had done everything I could, to the absolute best of my ability, to help them solve whatever dilemma they had been facing. If I wasn't able to resolve their issues at that moment, I assured them that I would find a source of information that could resolve them.

I know it works—because I've practiced my "you're the doctor, fix the problem" philosophy for more than twenty years, with great success.

Once you and your employees begin to think like doctors, you're going to be amazed at the differences, both in your workplace, and in the amount of new business that begins to come through your door.

But as the leader of your organization, it all begins with you! The success of your business lies in your hands—and you can achieve that success by beginning now to offer your customers superior customer service.

Throughout this book, the mantra will be: "You're the doctor, so fix the problem!"

Easy Strategies and Concepts

In this book you'll be learning how to successfully get both you and your employees to start thinking in a different way when it comes to dealing with your customers. You'll also be learning about proven concepts and strategies that have worked for many people in all sectors of the business world. From CEO's looking to make widespread changes within their company in order to provide better service for their customers, to managers trying to change the thinking patterns of their staff and create a team mentality and increased morale for their employees, these strategies have been proven to get amazing results.

There's no difficult hidden secret or magic to what you're going to be reading. The key factor is to get yourself and your staff to begin thinking in a new way. Once everyone in your organization begins to think like a doctor, things are going to start improving in a positive way for you and your company.

Let's Get Started

Always remember: it takes more than just good products and good customer service to be successful in today's business climate—it takes good products and great customer service!

And providing great customer service involves teaching every employee this phrase: "You're the doctor, so fix the problem!"

1

You're the Doctor, So Fix the Problem!

It's important to remember that, first and foremost, every business in the world, no matter what field it might be in, is really in the customer service business It doesn't matter whether you're working for McDonald's, Wendy's, Nordstrom's, Sears, Wal-Mart; a secretary, a salesperson, or CEO; of a company that is among the Fortune 500—if you're in business, you're in the customer service business.

Why the Doctor?

Throughout this book, we're going to be using doctor analogies, but perhaps it's not immediately obvious why I believe the practice of medicine to be the closest analogy to good customer service. So let's look at the similarities more closely. Both doctors and conscientious customer service representatives are dedicated to finding solutions to people's problems. (In that light, I suppose you could say that doctors are sort of in the customer service industry on a double basis.)

Whether we're suffering from a severe cold or in need of major surgery, doctors are the people we count on to offer expert help. We go to doctors for concerns and issues dealing with both our minds and bodies—problems we may not understand or know how to solve on our own—and we expect our doctor be familiar with our problem and to give us the answer we're seeking.

Every day in America, millions of customers turn to their customer service representatives for exactly the same reasons. They have encountered a concern or issue they generally can't solve on their own, for various reasons, so they turn to a customer service professional for expert advice.

That's why I'll be using the doctor/patient analogy throughout this book when offering examples of how to offer your clients great customer service.

Everyone Can Relate

For the first couple of chapters, we'll be talking about the concept of thinking like a doctor, and how that relates to great customer service. Simply telling your people that they're empowered to make their own decision on how to best deal with your customers isn't enough, because the term empowered is intangible. But when you teach your employees to think like doctors, the concept comes to life. After all, everyone has had experience with doctors, and they've seen first-hand what it means to have someone totally focused on solving their needs or concerns—and that is what great customer service is all about!

Finding Common Ground

Ninety percent of the time, you should be able to solve your client's issues, even if it only means listening to their concerns and then offering expert advice. It doesn't matter what industry you're in, your customers come to you for help in solving their issues and to get answers about finding the things they want.

If you always remember that when customers walk through your door, they're seeking answers to needs and concerns, just like patients visiting a doctor's office, your success rate will always be above average—and if you're able to maintain a 90% solution rate, your company's success will be just as good as the doctor's office. It's an achievable goal, and you are going to be reading how to do that in this book.

The added bonuses are many. Your customers will be satisfied, which means they will also return the next time they have a need or experience a problem—and they'll tell their associates about the positive experience with your company, which is the finest advertising a business can ask for!

When a family moves to a new town, one of their first tasks is to find a good doctor, and when they find one who is efficient, knowledgeable, and fits their family's personality style, they'll stick with that doctor until circumstances change. They'll be loyal to that doctor, and won't change unless either they move away or the doctor closes up shop. They trust that person, and wouldn't dream of changing, so long as the doctor continues to correctly maintain the family's health. They'll also tell friends about their positive experiences, which will bring more patients to the doctor's clientele.

It works the exact same way in the customer service field. If you give your clients great customer service on a continuing basis, they'll stick with you, remain loyal, and tell their associates, which will increase your business. So, in a very real way, you are the doctor within your field of expertise, and whatever business you're involved in, you're just as important to your customers as patients' doctors are to them.

It's an ongoing process, and you'll need to maintain your high level of problem solving in order to keep your customers coming back. Your customers will have a wide variety of questions they'll want answered—both before they make a purchase, and after that purchase has been made—just as a patient does when contemplating surgery and then during the recovery process.

How Doctors Approach Great Customer Service

What if a customer asks a question that you literally can't answer? It's not the time to panic—it's the time to get resourceful and prove to your customer that you truly are committed to providing superior customer service! Thinking like a doctor, you first instinct will be to find someone within your organization who does know the answer to the customer's question, and if that fails, you'll look outside your organization for answers. Remember, the customer doesn't care what resources you tap into to solve their issues—they just want them solved.

A situation like that brings us back to our doctor analogy. When doctors run up against a situation that's unfamiliar or baffling to them, what do they do? They immediately seek out the help of a specialist in the field of medicine that deals with whatever problem they've encountered.

Doctors don't fake knowledge—doing that could prove fatal to their patients Instead, when they don't know the answer, they turn to someone who can help find the correct answer for them. So always remember, remind your employees on a daily basis: you're the doctor, so fix the problem! When a customer comes in the door with a tough problem, find a way to fix it, and if you can't fix it personally, seek out someone who can. In the end, the result will be exactly the same—a satisfied customer.

Tough Days Turned Good

In order to be effective at your job, whatever it may be, you must begin to be completely honest—with yourself, your coworkers, and your customers. If you don't feel good about yourself or our position at your place of business, it will reflect in your attitude toward everyone with whom you come into contact.

You also can't let frustration, anger, or a bad mood affect your job performance If you find yourself getting testy with your customers, a great deal of the time it won't be the customer that's triggering your negative feelings Your anger has probably been building up for some time, and has nothing to do with your clients, so you must guard against taking your frustration out on them Your customers never deserve to be treated with anything but the utmost respect and honesty.

It's important to be honest about your real source of anger and frustration. First, admit that you are frustrated, and then try to determine the root cause of your negative feelings, whether it be job-related or home-related. Then, once you've identified the source of your negative feelings, set those feelings aside when dealing with your customers. Focus on your client's problems, find out what their needs are, and then set out to meet those needs.

Though it might sound counterintuitive, helping your customers can actually be cathartic, offering you a chance to forget, at least for awhile, about your negative issues while you're concentrating all your efforts into helping someone else. Concentrating solely on your customers can be a great way to cruise through a day, no matter which rung of the corporate ladder you occupy. You'll be so caught up in giving your clients excellent customer service that before you know it, your work day will be over—and you'll find that it was actually a pretty good one, at that! All of your customers walked away happy, and you'll have a sense of accomplishment that will improve your confidence in your ability to deal with your other difficulties. When you find yourself in a funk at work, it's worthwhile to rearrange your thinking.

Stop being the patient, and remember that you're the doctor! Your customers have sought you out for help, which is an honor in itself, and they have confidence that you're both willing and able to solve their concerns and needs. So let your frustration and anger go, and concentrate instead on being the doctor.

What if you were scheduled for an operation and your surgeon was frustrated with some area of their life? If you're scheduled to be the patient in this scenario, you certainly don't want to be put under the knife by someone who is unstable, angry, and frustrated.

So what happens on the day you show up for your operation? Regardless of what your surgeon is feeling about their life, you're going to see them smiling, and offering you encouragement about the surgery in a reassuring voice. If that surgeon has problems, you'll never know about them as a patient. Doctors and surgeons know how to separate their own personal problems from those of their patients.

You can use that attitude to help you become much more effective in your own job, whatever it may be. It doesn't matter if you're not in the position you'd ultimately like to be within your company. If you concentrate on taking care of your customers, one by one, you're going to keep moving forward—

there's no way to stop that positive momentum. But it only happens by giving your very best, one day and one customer at a time.

Never look down on yourself or the job you're currently holding. Every position in every company is important to that business's ultimate success—and that includes your job! So you owe it to yourself, your family, and your company to do your current job in the best, most effective way possible. No matter what it may be, your job is important, and you are important—so do your job well, by focusing on your customers and their needs, and by gaining more knowledge about your products and services every day. It will pay off later, I promise.

You're the doctor, so fix the problem.

Don't get too caught up in your feelings, because feelings are just that—feelings! Feelings are not facts. So whatever feelings you're having on any given day, always remember that they'll eventually pass, whether they're good and bad.

If you're having a great day and you're feeling as if nothing can go wrong, by all means, go with those good feelings, pass your enthusiasm along to your customers and fellow employees, and you'll get even more enthusiasm in return. That's the great thing about spreading good feelings—they come back with even greater rewards.

On the other hand, the exact same principle applies when it comes to passing on negative feelings. That's why it's so important to get a handle on the source of your anger and frustration before you begin spreading those negative feelings to your customers and coworkers. Before that happens, you have to stop, be honest about where your anger is coming from, and then get it in check, before you take it out on the wrong person—like your customer, fellow employee, or boss!

But how do you do that? There are a number of ways. If it's possible, take a two or three minute walk—away from everyone—outside, if you can Such power walks are good for regrouping and regaining control. If you can't take a walk, try heading to the lunchroom or even the restroom—anywhere that allows you to step away from your current situation and try to come to grips with the cause of your negative emotions.

The important thing is to do it right away, so you can clear your mind—like a doctor in between patients—before turning your attention to the next customer or issue at hand. Stop, regroup, identify the problem, let it go, and then move on to the next task.

You're the doctor—fix the problem.

That's what this book is designed to do: to help you begin to think of yourself as a doctor within your workplace, someone who is constantly working to help those patients who have sought you out for help and advice. Read each chapter as if your job success—and that of your company—depended on it, because it does. Pass the information on to your employees, because everyone in your organization, from top to bottom, should be constantly looking for ways to improve their level of customer service. When you're finished with this book, the principles you'll be putting into action in your life will yield results that will amaze you!

If the concepts seem difficult at first, don't get discouraged. New ways of thinking don't come easy, keep in mind that we're not looking for perfection in the beginning—all you're hoping for is to make improvements, one step at a time. So stay with me as we work our way through the process of rearranging your thought processes in a positive way.

All are Critical to Success

Since you're the doctor, let's take a moment to scrub up, clear your mind, and prepare for the next step toward your ultimate success. Remember, as we said earlier, every person in every job of every company is really in the customer service business. (And if you extend the concept out even further, we're all in the customer service business in life as a whole, for that matter.)

The first step is to let go of your pride! No matter what position you currently hold in your company, there should be no shame, and no head held too high in the sky From the person with the smallest title to the one with the longest string of words in his job description, each person is critical to making a good company better In reality, though the concept is often hard for upper division managers and owners to swallow, every person in the company is really doing the same job—serving the customer. Each person in the business is serving others, in the hope that those people will then both return to the company and tell others about the superior service they received That's really what it's all about. Sure, there's a product or service involved, but in the end, it's customer service that will ultimately spell the difference between a company's success or failure.

Great customer service comes easiest when you feel good about yourself, and when everyone around you feels good, as well. So whether you're at the top of the totem pole or the bottom, respect all of your customers and fellow employees. That will make them feel good about themselves, and in turn, they'll pass that feeling along to everyone with whom they come into contact.

To achieve such good feelings about yourself, your customers, and your company, begin looking at each task of every day as a stepping stone toward your ultimate success Begin to go out of your way to make an extra effort to treat every customer as if they were the key to the fulfillment of your dream and success—because they are, no matter what that ultimate dream or success may be!

Don't worry about who gets the promotions or makes the most money within your company. If you continue to stay positive and give an added measure of service to every customer and coworker, your promotions will come soon enough—it's guaranteed!

If you see someone who seems to be rapidly moving up through the chain of command, don't become envious or frustrated. Instead, begin to watch that person carefully, and take note of the extra little things they do to give their customers better service. You'll find that you can learn a lot from observing successful people. Then you can take that knowledge and put it to work in your own quest for success.

On the other end of the spectrum, if you happen to be at the top of your company's roster, walk into your place of business as if you were "one of the gang." Be friendly, smile, and greet employees by name whenever possible. Remember, you can give your employees a great deal of respect and still hold them accountable. In fact, offering your employees added respect will actually encourage them to become more accountable.

No one likes to be put down. If you, as an employer, fail to instill a sense of dignity, respect, and team spirit in your employees, you'll find your turnover rate is going to increase— and no matter how you look at it; employee turnover is not a good thing.

In fact, employee turnover affects not just your company, but your customers, as well. Customers notice when there's a new face replacing the old one they had come to know and trust, and it takes time for that new employee to establish a rapport with a customer—and that "getting to know each other" time frame is a perfect time for your competition to step in and lure that customer away.

A high turnover rate also suggests to your customers that all is not right within your company. Your regular clients will ask employees what happened to the person they had normally dealt with, and the answers they get may not always reflect well on your company's image. I've seen this situation first-hand, and it can be devastating to a client's perception of a company—which can affect business in a profoundly negative way.

In summary, it's important to remember that we're all in the customer service industry, so give your clients the best you've got, and your company will grow—as will your personal dreams. Look at every task of every day as a stepping stone toward your next level of success, and go out of your way to treat every customer as if they held the key to your next promotion If you already hold a high position on the corporate ladder, treat your employees fairly, and with respect and dignity.

In short, begin to think like a doctor.

Whatever needs, concerns or problem your client has come to you for, recognize that they are honoring you by believing you can provide the answer—so do everything in your power to find that answer. You're the doctor, so fix the problem—and if you can't solve it yourself, find a specialist who can help!

These concepts may all be new to you, but when you begin to rearrange your thought patterns and think like a doctor, you'll start to achieve new levels of success for yourself and your company almost immediately!

And it all boils down to a simple formula: you're the doctor, so fix the problem!

2

What Makes a Good Company Better?

Before we get started, take a moment to clear your mind of everything you've learned in the past about customer service, in order to make room for the new information you're about to read. We're going to be rearranging your thinking patterns, until you can't imagine thinking any other way except like the doctor you are within your field of business. Then you're going to pass this concept on to each and every one of your employees, helping them to truly understand how important their jobs are to the overall organization, and how every decision they make will affect the company's ultimate success or failure.

So take a few moments to let your mind grow quiet, and begin to imagine yourself as a general practitioner, a person whose sole purpose in life is to help people achieve total satisfaction every time they come to you for advice and treatment for their concerns and needs.

In order to perform your duties as a doctor most effectively, it's important that you allow your mind to clear in between patients. You need to completely let go of the issues your previous client had, as well as the steps you took to resolve those issues. None of that will matter to your next patient, since they're only concerned with what is going on in their lives, and the issues they're dealing with. Every client will bring unique wants and needs to the table, which you'll need to address specifically, focusing your energy entirely on their needs and concerns. Only when that's been achieved can you be certain that you'll be giving every customer, great customer service.

The Key Factor

When your mind is clear and receptive, you'll be able to listen intently as each new patient/customer begins to speak. You can focus on what they're saying about their needs, and once you've completely heard them out, you'll have a much clearer notion as to how you can best provide the relief they're hoping to find.

Thinking as a doctor, you can see how important listening is if you're going to create a successful business. So, bearing all that in mind, let's look at what makes one business stand out from its competition, and what makes one company better than another?

Take a moment to really think about the question. Open your mind and expand your thoughts, making an honest comparison between your company and your competition Ask yourself what it is that makes a customer prefer one store over another, even if both stores carry the exact same products, and why some people are so fiercely loyal to a certain business, even though there are dozens of competitors listed in the Yellow Pages under the same category.

I'm sure some ideas will immediately come to mind, but if not, perhaps you'll want to stop reading for a few moments, put the book down, and give the issue some genuine thought. After all, the success of your company depends on your answers to these important questions. How can you make your company stand out from its competition?

From my experience of the past two decades in the customer service industry, and from talking with thousands of customers, owners, and managers about what makes one company rise above its competition, the answer that comes up again and again is great customer service.

But in order to be effective, a company's customer service program must go far beyond the short term. Getting your customers to prefer your business over others in the same field involves thinking long-term, and in terms of satisfying your clients—who will then return to your place of business for the same great customer service. They'll also tell their friends, family, and acquaintances about the wonderful customer service they received, which gives your company the very best form of advertising, which is having customers tell the world about their exceptional experience.

Great customer service—it's the number one reason why customers choose one company over another, even when both companies sell the same products It sounds simple, but knowing the answer to the question is only the beginning Now you must find a way to facilitate that concept into your everyday dealings with our customers and employees.

Great Customer Service or Price Wars?

For many years, I've watched various companies struggle with trying to improve their position in the marketplace, and there are two basic strategies for trying to accomplish that goal. The first involves trying to gain an advantage over the competition by cutting prices and engaging in an all-out price war.

There's no doubt that customers will be quite happy with the price war strategy, at least in the beginning—and the company's initial bottom line might look good for a while, when the first quarterly profit/loss statements come in. But the price war strategy also comes with a heavy cost to the company, especially when it's not coupled with a commitment to superior customer service, which is a difficult balance to achieve, as you'll see as we continue in this chapter.

For many companies, especially smaller companies, engaging in the price war game can prove to be fatal. When a company chooses such a strategy, other parts of the business will soon begin to suffer, since it's often the customer service end of the business that ends up taking the first hit, because employees are often too busy restocking shelves to really focus on customer needs. Not focusing squarely on customers sets off a domino-like chain of events that will ultimately turn a company into just another failure statistic.

When profit margins are small, a company's overhead must be reduced, and one way that's typically done is by paying employees less—but that strategy can often prove disastrous. Earning less money means that employee loyalty is reduced. If they were better paid and not so overworked, employees would take greater pride in their jobs, because knowing that their employer values them enough to pay an above average wage, coupled with having the time to engage in more meaningful interactions with customers makes for a much more pleasant work environment.

When a company is involved in the price war game, that company's poorly-paid employees are simply working for their meager paycheck from week to week, and they have no real incentive to care about either the company or its customers After all, it's just a paycheck—it's not a career—it's just something to do until they can find a better-paying situation.

It's also been shown that employees who are poorly paid are much more likely to steal from the company, which further erodes a business's bottom line Regardless of what type of high-tech security systems management may install, employees who have no stake in the company will find ways to pilfer goods and merchandise from their employer. One of the consequences of those increased security measures is that companies must fire more employees who are caught stealing and then spend money retraining their replacements—as well as incurring the costs of prosecuting the thieves, which erodes the bottom line even further.

Engaging in the all-out price war technique is one of the biggest reasons why small companies have historically come and gone within just five to ten years in this country. If the employees don't care, because it seems as if the company doesn't care about them, the business will fail—period. I've seen it happen again and again over the years, and the most important thing to understand is that it doesn't have to be that way.

The Route to Great Customer Service

Now let's take a look at what happens when a company focuses their attention on providing superior customer service instead of just cutting prices! It's not necessarily the easiest way, but companies that have focused on great customer service are always the ones that show the greatest success rate, and quickly rise above their competition, regardless of what business they're in.

Providing great customer service means taking a caring and thoughtful attitude toward everyone involved, but it begins by having each employee in the organization let go of the "me" attitude. To be successful, every person involved in the company must think of themselves as part of a team and being a doctor, capable of fixing any problem for any customer at any time—no better or worse than any other team member within the organization.

That can prove to be the hardest part of the program for managers and supervisors to buy into, but they must, if the company is to succeed. If a company's employees feel as if they're just as valuable to the overall success of the business as top management, or anyone else, they'll always keep the best interests of the company in mind. That's why the doctor concept is so effective—it gives employees a sense of self-worth, knowing they're a valued member of a team. After all, caring about the company's success is also in the best interest of the employees and their family's future.

As the owner or head of a company, one of the wisest business decisions you can make is to encourage your employees to care about your company as if they were part owners themselves. It's a simple concept, reminding each employee to think like a doctor and fix each customer's problem they encounter, and letting them know that they will be held fully accountable for their actions at all times If you do that, your employees will work harder and more efficiently, and will treat customers with a greater degree of respect—all of which will improve both morale and profits, and will automatically make your company stand out from your competitors.

In the beginning of the chapter, we asked why some customers repeatedly shop at one store, even though a competitor may offer the same merchandise, sometimes at slightly better prices. In a nutshell, the answer to our original question is simple: courteous, caring, and empowered employees!

So what is it that will make a good company better? It's the fruits of its employees' labor, and how they conceive themselves within the framework of the company will directly affect how employees treat that company's customers.

Of course, I'm not suggesting that a competitive price for goods or services isn't important to a company's overall success. To be truly successful, a company must offer a combination of both good prices and excellent customer service, and if you can do that—and you can—you'll be well on your way toward profit and success.

As you move through the ideas and concepts you're going to find in this book, you're going to learn how to achieve the best balance between price and customer service. You'll learn how to punch in the numbers, make calls to vendors, and then to take advantage of the best wholesale prices for your merchandise But at the same time, you're going to learn how to balance those numbers against an intangible, but vastly more important factor for your business's success—outstanding customer service.

3

Standing Firm with Accountability

We're going to begin this chapter by looking at the most important factor in any company's customer service policy—standing firm with accountability But first, always thinking like doctors, we're going to scrub up.

Take a moment to clear your mind as you prepare to read this chapter. Take a couple minutes to really think about what the term accountability really means to you and to everyone else in your organization. You may think you are holding others accountable for their actions and words, but are you also doing the same thing for yourself?

It's been said before, but the best way to lead really is by example.

In that light, here are a few questions to ask yourself—and remember, this isn't a test, and no one but you will know your answers, so it's all right to be totally honest. In fact, that's the only way you're going to be able to improve the quality of your company's customer service After all, the one person in the world you must be completely truthful with, above all others, is yourself.

Are You Accountable?

Do you hold firm when it comes to accountability for whatever job you're responsible for in your organization?

Do you ever "pass the buck," so that if something should go wrong, the responsibility won't fall onto your shoulders?

Have you ever heard about a negative situation within your organization that could have been avoided if you had taken the responsibility to address it?

Are you holding others accountable, but not yourself?

Do you simply assume that someone else will complete a particular job, using the excuse that you're simply "too busy?"

Are you involved with your organization? (I mean truly involved.)

Do you believe that you have a genuine stake in the overall success of your business?

I know, these are hard questions, and some of your answers may have made you uncomfortable But without accountability— and I mean real, true accountability—you're giving away the control of your organization.

But let's not stop there. If you think that sounds bad, let's look into our crystal ball and see what the future will hold if you don't become accountable for your company's success.

Little by little—and possibly a lot by a lot, if you really don't take care of business—your company's profits will begin to dwindle Then, unless the situation changes dramatically, your customers are going to seek out a competitor who knows what true accountability and exceptional customer service really means.

I'm sure that when you started with your company, at whatever level that may have been, you had all sorts of great ideas and lots of profit in mind—for yourself and for the entire company. But as time goes on, the tendency of every employee, at every level, is to get so busy with the million-and-one things that need to be done on a daily basis just to keep the company doors open, which leaves less and less time for doing the innovative and consumer-oriented things that will continue to lift your business above your competition.

But that is a huge mistake, and ignoring your company's real number one asset—your customers—can be a death sentence to a business, no matter how efficiently that company may be run on a day-to-day basis.

A Look into the Future

Continuing with our look into the crystal ball:

As you continue to give away the control of your company by not demanding accountability from every single employee—and yourself—you also begin to lose control of your customers! You look at the profit/loss numbers every day, and you begin to see that something is definitely not right. The profits are shrinking, but you can't quite put your finger on the reason. Your product hasn't changed—there may have even been some significant improvement or a new line may have been introduced that is superior to your competition, but it hasn't improved the bottom line. It just doesn't make sense, and you find yourself becoming more and more concerned about your company's health and long-term prospects.

Then, you begin to realize that there have been more complaints from customers that seem to have nothing directly to do with your product line. The number of complaints might not be of epidemic proportions, but it seems to be increasing.

Although you look at many aspects of the company for clues as to why profits are down, you slowly begin to understand that your employees aren't being held accountable for dealing with the company's customers in the most efficient, caring manner.

Then it finally dawns on you: an organization's success or failure ultimately depends on providing superior customer service—which begins with accountability, at every level of the company.

But what does that mean? Each employee must treat the company's customers with courtesy and kindness, and strive to make sure that every transaction ends with a satisfied customer. Employees must be accountable for their actions, words, and attitudes—every day, and in every situation.

The bottom line: superior customer service and true employee accountability go hand-in-hand when it comes to creating and maintaining a successful organization. I've seen it time and time again—companies that diligently go to work on improving their customer service and employee accountability issues very quickly begin to see significant changes in their overall profits. But it all begins with making every employee in the organization totally accountable. Think like doctors, who are always totally accountable to their patients for their actions—are you doing the same for your customers?

Accountability: Simple Put, It's Important!

This chapter has been a short one, because there should be no long discussion about what it means to be accountable. Being totally accountable is a simple concept, and allowing your employees to be totally accountable for their actions gives them the tools they need to provide your customers with great customer service. There are several key factors involved in improving customer service, and we're going to look at them in more detail as we move along. But they all begin with standing firm with accountability.

So, like a doctor between patients, clear your thoughts about what you've just read, open your mind, and let's begin learning some more valuable lessons in how to create outstanding customer service.

4

The Hidden Back Door

All right, doctor, let's move on to the next phase of your quest for superior customer service. Again, your first task is to scrub up, and then begin to prepare yourself for your next patient. That means letting go of what has just happened previously, relaxing your mind, and allowing yourself to become open to whatever new information that's about to come your way.

Like all doctors do, it's important for you to clear your thoughts after each transaction with a customer or issue has been completed. By clearing your mind of all the thoughts and emotions that just took place, you'll be making sure that you'll be open and receptive to whatever situation will be arising next, and you'll be better able to hear and understand your next issue, employee or customer concern. In turn, being able focus on your new customer's needs and desires will then allow you to take the appropriate action to address those concerns quickly and effectively.

It may be an old cliché, but it's as true today as it ever has been (and perhaps even more so): every business succeeds by helping one customer at a time. Following that sage advice is easy: take care of every single customer who comes into contact with your organization, and your company will continue to grow—pure and simple.

What You'll Seldom See or Hear About

In this chapter, we're going begin discussing how to take care of every customer, but this time, we're going to take a bit different approach. During this discussion, we'll be talking about what you, as the boss, will seldom see or hear about.

We're talking about the customer who walked away from your business unsatisfied Their experience was not pleasant, and if you were to ask them, they'd have a simple, two-word answer to sum up their dealings with your establishment.

They'd shake their heads and say, "It sucked!"

That may be a rather ineloquent way to put it, but there's no doubt that their statement adequately sums up their feelings about the way they were treated during their last visit—and about your entire company, as a result.

Here's the scenario:

The customer originally came into your place of business with a genuine need, searching for products or service they hope your company provides. They had tried to solve it themselves but weren't able to, so they turned to your organization for expert help and advice.

However, when they came face-to-face with one of your company's representatives, they didn't get the respect and helpful advice they needed to solve their dilemma. Finally, when they walked away from that interaction, they not only were frustrated, but they also were determined never to return.

Unless something drastic happens, your company won't ever see that customer again. Depending on their personality type or level of frustration, that customer may not complain by writing a letter to the company or making a phone call, so management will never hear about how frustrated and unhappy they were. If the customer just decides to drop the entire matter—and any future dealings with your company—you, as the head of the organization, will never know what happened.

That unfortunate scenario leads to a situation I call the hidden back door.

In business, there are few things that travel faster or have more impact than word of mouth, and that unhappy customer will suddenly become the most effect form of advertising against your company that you can imagine.

Statistics show that an unhappy customer will tell at least three other people about their negative experience with a company. In turn, each of those people will tell several others, and before long, the amount of negativity in the story has increased, getting bigger and bigger each time it's passed on— and your company's bottom line will suffer as a result.

It's a bit like the old game of "telephone," in which a group of people pass along a story from person to person, until the final person announces what they have ultimately heard at the end of the line. Invariably, that final statement bears little or no resemblance to the original story that was whispered at the beginning of the game.

That's exactly what happens with negative word of mouth. The story may have little truth left by the time a potential client hears it, but it doesn't matter. It came to them from a person they trust to be reliable, so it's taken as gospel—and can hurt your company's reputation in a powerful way.

Let's Do the Math

If you have ten customers every month who walk out of your establishment unsatisfied, and they each tell three friends, that's at least thirty potential customers that will be lost—each and every month. And that's only the first level in the downward word of mouth spiral! That number could easily triple by the time the cycle was complete!

An unsatisfied customer can do more to harm your company's reputation than almost any other factor. When a potential client, who may be looking for exactly the product or service your company provides, hears negative things about your organization, they may decide not to even give you the opportunity to serve them.

When your company gets caught in this downward spiral, your choices as the head person become limited. You might find that lowering your prices will help for a while, but low prices alone won't be enough to keep your business afloat if you're not also taking excellent care of your customers.

Throughout history, it's been proven that customers will gladly pay slightly more for goods and services that are also backed by superior customer service, which a few good companies are offering, and this is the time for you and your company to become one of those superior companies, drawing in and keeping those customers It just involves getting everyone in your organization to think like a doctor, constantly holding themselves totally accountable and sincerely seeking solutions to customer wants and needs (which is really just another way to say "providing excellent customer service).

Having spent more than twenty years in the customer service industry myself, I've seen this scenario over and over. Companies seek profits by lowering their prices, but fail to take excellent care of their customers—and that company fails. It may take a number of years for that company to go under, depending upon what type of financial backing they initially may have had, but they eventually fail, nonetheless.

Never Forget This Simple Fact

Satisfied customers are the lifeblood of your company, and taking care of each customer is vital to your organization's success—period.

Taking good care of your customers involves holding every employee in your company completely accountable, from top to bottom. If an employee happens to be in a bad mood, unhappy with their supervisor or not quite all there due to a bit too much partying the night before, it will reflect negatively on your entire company in a customer's mind.

Another situation that will prompt negative customer feelings is when a company is obviously short-staffed. Short-staffing means that lines back up and inadequate attention is given to customer needs, causing both customers and employees to become unhappy. Then, when a customer's turn to be helped finally does arrive, employees aren't able to spend enough time with them.

All of those factors will register negatively in a client's mind, and will give them the clear impression that your company doesn't care enough about its customers to make certain that their visit is a pleasant experience. It also tells them, in no uncertain terms, that instead of making it the top priority, that company has placed its most valuable asset—its customers—last on their list.

If you want your company to succeed, don't let your customers keep walking out the hidden back door. It can ultimately sound the death knell for your organization If your company's profit/loss numbers begin to slide, the very first place to look for improvement is in how your precious customers are being treated If they're not being treated exceptionally well, it's time to make some significant changes—and fast!

How do you begin making the changes necessary to improve your company's customer service? Well, you've already taken the first important step: you're reading this book!

The next step is to close the hidden back door. If your company is going to be successful, it's crucial for each and every customer to enter your establishment through the front door and then leave through that same door—and the only way that's going to happen is if every customer walks away from their interaction with your company's employees with a smile on their face.

Close the hidden back door, and your customers will suddenly become the most effective positive advertising for your company. The word of mouth formula will then begin to work to your company's advantage, and not to its detriment.

Repeat customers will keep your business going, even during tough times, and the more satisfied your customers are, the more likely they'll be to tell their friends and associates about their pleasant experience. That will generate more revenue, and will signal a long life and happy times for your company.

Every single one of us is a consumer, and when we find a product or service that suits our needs, backed by superior customer service, we're not only pleased, but we'll recommend the company that made us feel that way to everyone we know. We'll also continue to shop with that company for as long as they're in business—or as long as they continue to make our shopping a satisfying experience.

How does that translate to any company's bottom line?

More money, more money, and more money.

In the next chapter, we'll begin laying out a step-by-step strategy for closing the hidden back door—forever.

5

Interaction

Now it's time to get down to basics, and first of all, as you begin this chapter, I want you to forget about expensive software and being overwhelmed by 1000-page customer service manuals. Accountability and interaction in American business has gotten much too far away from true interaction between company employees and customers.

Technology Can't Replace Interaction

Many companies have and are trying to replace personal interaction with modern technology, in the hope that it will solve their customer service issues and save money, but from my years on the front line with customers and from being on the other side as a customer, I'm here to tell you that's not what happens.. By the time companies have added in all the lost revenue from alienated customers, that practice simply doesn't make sense.

Now don't get me wrong. I believe that modern technology is a very good thing in most cases, especially when it comes to increasing efficiency, but when it comes to the interaction between company employees and customers, technology definitely isn't the answer. If you have doubts about that, just think back to how many times a real person could have resolved your customer service issue in the time it took for you to sit on the phone, waiting to get results from a computer.

So technology is good for some business applications, but not for others—but let's examine the reasons.

First, technology upgrades are very expensive in themselves, and when the cost of training employees to operate that technology and the added cost of maintenance, the overall cost can be enormous.

Second, computers can't be held accountable, which, as we discussed in the last chapter, is crucial to a company's ultimate success. We can blame computer programmers or the people who operate them, but in the end, no one is held directly accountable when a computer error occurs—and the customer continues to be unhappy with your services, which means that the negative word of mouth that we've discussed begins to erode the company's image. Technology has its place in business, there's no doubt about that. But if you're thinking about upgrading your company's technology, use it for anything but interacting with your customers—because you've got far too much to lose in the long run.

For example, think about when you have to call most companies today for some sort of customer service issue. Trying to reach a real person becomes a real time-consuming, frustrating event. Since most people have busy schedules, being on hold for twenty minutes represents the worst type of customer service. There are a few exceptions, and there are some companies who have gone back to the use of live human beings, rather than forcing customers to punch in an endless string of numbers before finally getting to talk to a real person. Being able to speak to a live representative within two or three rings is a great step toward providing superior customer service.

You're the doctor, so fix the problem.

Natural Born Leaders

Are you a leader or a follower? Don't answer too quickly, because the fact is, in order to be most effective, the best leaders are those who also know how to follow. If you're the leader of your company, you're ultimately responsible for where you and your company are going, so if you choose someone to follow, you'd better choose carefully, and follow other leaders who truly know where they're going.

In the end, you're the only one who can get yourself on the right path—whether it's in your business life or your life in general. To do that, you must start by being totally honest with your followers, because only by letting them know exactly where they stand and where they're headed can your followers make good, informed choices.

Now I'm not saying that you should try to be a psychic. Being a leader doesn't mean that you always will know exactly where you're going to end up—that's not possible, given the vagaries of the economy. But being honest with yourself and everyone else is a great start toward getting on the right path. You do all of this in tiny increments—one step at a time—through making sure you have excellent interaction with both customers and employees.

In the last chapter, I promised to offer you the solution for closing the hidden back door. Well, here it is, and it can be summed up in just one word: interaction.

That's it, in a nutshell. The key to closing the hidden back door, and to creating a highly motivated work force, is interaction—from the CEO on down to the janitors who clean up the building on the night shift. Of course, it's easier said than done, but effective interaction must be in place throughout the company in order for the organization to work well and to continue to attract repeat customers.

As we begin to show you how to implement a new interaction program in your company, keep in mind that the process doesn't require micro-management. In fact, resorting to micro-management will actually undermine the program, lowering employee morale and lessening their ability to deal effectively with customers. Instead, you want to empower your employees to address the issues that arise between the company and its customers–and the best way to do that is to get them to start thinking like doctors.

You're the doctor, so fix the problem.

It all begins with trust. You need to trust your employees to make the right decisions, and once they've been given the training we'll be offering in this book, they'll know and understand what to do in any given situation. (That, too, can be summed up in a simple phrase: "The customer is always right.")

Empowering your employees also carries an inherent responsibility, as well. If employees are empowered, that means they must know that they'll also be held accountable for their actions and interactions. Let every employee know that they're valuable to the overall organization, and as long as they continue to give the customers great service, they can look forward to not only continued employment, but also a chance to move up in the company. But all employees must understand that the customer always comes first.

No one wants to be just a body in a job or a just a single cog in an impersonal machine You're looking for employees who will stay with the company, and people love their jobs when they're made to feel important to the overall organization.

Pay Your Customers and Employees Forward

When it comes to interaction, it's important to lead by example, and that leadership must start with the person at the top. So from this point on, you must begin teaching your employees to give excellent customer service, which begins with the concept of paying forward, in order to receive even greater benefit later. This isn't a concept that's understood or practiced by many people, but it works, and works well, whether in a business context or in a person's life.

Again, you'll need to begin by showing, rather than telling, your employees how the concept works. Start by taking some time out of your busy schedule to get to know your employees. For many folks in management positions, this will be a totally new idea, but it's vital for the success of the program.

As you get to know your people, you'll begin to see a shift in their attitudes The ones who already have a positive outlook toward their jobs and the company will be even more energized, and the employees who previously were simply going through the motions will begin to show renewed interest in providing customers with better service.

The second part of your program is to get to know your customers more thoroughly, with the aim of making every customer a repeat customer. Just like the employees, there will be some customers who are more enthusiastic about the process than others. That's because they are all people first, and employees or customers second. But every one of them is important to your company's success, bringing in the revenue that will keep the doors open for years to come.

That is what we mean when we talk about paying forward. It doesn't matter if you don't fully understand how it all works The only thing that matters is that it does, and that which you pay forward will come back to you, ten times over.

Increasing your interaction doesn't mean calling every employee into your office or walking through the building shaking hands as if you were running for some type of public office. You already have the title. What you're doing is trying to help your employees follow our thoughts and dreams—not by memo, but by genuine interaction!

You can interact meaningfully with your employees by working alongside them for as little as 15 minutes. That time may not seem like much, but the interaction you have with that employee will make a huge impression, and will prompt a significant change in that person's attitude and morale.

Remember, this isn't a race, and it isn't an election. What you're doing is trying to instill a sense of commitment in every employee by letting them know that you are committed to knowing them and trying to understand their thoughts and feelings about their job. By spending even a token amount of time with each employee, you're demonstrating your own lifetime commitment to improving your company.

Some companies are larger than others, of course, but that's fine. No matter how large your company may be, you can break it down into smaller segments, spending a certain amount of time with each person in your organization, one at a time, to demonstrate your sincerity about improving company morale and commitment to superior customer service. If your company is huge, the process will just take longer—but the basic process remains the same. It will take work, but it's entirely possible, and the results can be stunning.

One company I know designates one day a month and calls it "Customer Appreciation Day." On that day, 75% of the company's efforts are dedicated to getting to know their customers more thoroughly. All day, the supervisors walk through the work place, trying to talk with as many customers as possible, getting to know their names (remembering your customers' names is great PR, by the way), finding out why they have come into the store for, and what the company could do to improve their service. It's a terrific idea, and if you ask them, customers are fiercely loyal to that particular store, because they feel as if their opinions and their business are important. (Which they are!)

When you talk with customers, keep an open mind, because they'll tell you things that you might have never known otherwise—which will cause you to think about ways to improve your company's customer service. And that's really the main purpose for interacting with your customers—it gives you the opportunity to improve and grow.

As you talk to your customers, take notes on a pad or ask them if you can tape their comments on a mini-tape recorder. (That's also very good PR.) But most importantly, keep the mood light and don't take everything too seriously Never throw away any of the information you've gathered from your customers Whether the feedback was good or bad, there's always something to be learned from it.

Above all, be honest, and speak from your heart. Customers will remember honest, sincere interaction with the head of the company or management, and will keep coming back, because they feel as if they have friends in high places, should they ever experience a problem.

The "Customer Appreciation Day" concept could easily be adapted to an "Employee Appreciation Day," as well. It could take place one day a month, and would be a day in which management spent 75% of their time getting to know the employees on a more personal basis.

The concept is basically the same. You'll be doing the exact same thing that you did with your customers, except that you'll be talking to your employees After all, employees need to feel valuable to your company's success, too. (Because they are.) It's the way your employees treat your customers that determines whether those customers come back, or leave through the infamous hidden back door.

Train your employees to feel important and valuable to the overall organization, and show them that they're important by the way you interact with them every day. Let them know that you trust them to make wise decisions with your customers

Customers notice when there's lots of turnover in a company, and that's never good for your company's image. Customers, like all other human beings, are fond of stability.

They don't like to see too much change. They like to get to know the store and to be comfortable with its employees. There's nothing like walking into a store and seeing a familiar, friendly face. It inspires confidence in the present transaction, and for the future.

So, to create stability in your company, learn each employee's name, and what that person thinks about their job and about the company as a whole. Getting to know your employees will also help you keep an eye open for a potential superstar, since there's always one or two in every workplace.

Employees, and their interactions with your customers, are the lifeblood of your company, so get to know them as well as humanly possible. It means much more than you'll ever know—trust me, because I've been there. Employees will give their best effort when they know that the company cares for them, and that they have a chance for growth within the organization. But to do that, you must always maintain a team spirit. You want your employees to work as a team, and not as a group of individuals, fighting each other for the next promotion—and the best way to instill that team spirit is by interacting honestly with each employee.

Honesty is an absolute necessity, if you want to make the interaction process work. Your employees will respond to honesty, and will give you respect and trust in return.

As we've said a number of times before, and will say again: you're the doctor. So if your company is having difficulty with employee morale or customer relations, fix the problem.

This approach isn't taught in the MBA programs at any top university, but it's vital to your company's success. The more time you spend with your employees and customers in open and honest interaction, the more loyal they will become.

Interaction is the key to your company's success, and the sooner you begin to empower your employees to take better care of your customers, the sooner your company will begin a new phase of growth.

6

Presence

In this chapter, we're going to be talking about an all-important concept called presence. Presence is one of the most important aspects of providing superior customer service, because of the fact that first impressions are lasting impressions. But before we begin our discussion, like the doctors we are, we're going to scrub up, just as we always do before turning our attention to our next patient Take a few deep breaths and relax your mind in preparation for the new information you're about to read.

Take a moment or two to think about what the concept of presence means to you and how it affects your attitude when walk into a place of business, whether it's a department store, hardware store, restaurant, or doctor's office, and when you're ready, we'll begin. Think about how a company representative's appearance and product knowledge affects your overall shopping experience. Then move on to our discussion of the importance of establishing and maintaining a sense of professional presence in the marketplace.

First Impression

The chances are, when you first walk into a business establishment, the first thing you notice when you look around is the appearance of the personnel you encounter You notice whether each person representing the company is clean-cut, well-groomed, with their fingernails cut, and whether they're dressed appropriately for the job they're doing.

Although the world's opinion has changed considerably as to what is considered appropriate for employee work dress and appearance, customers still notice those things and are put off when a company's representative exhibits a less than professional image or a lack of product knowledge.

It may sound like a small thing, but I know from my years of experience in the customer service industry that customers do notice and are affected by those types of things and it can make a considerable difference in both their buying decisions and their overall impression of a company. In fact, many customers I've interviewed over the years have told me that an employee's presence was a key factor of making their experience at a place of business enjoyable and satisfying.

Here's an example from my own experience, but from the customer's side of the equation. One day, I was looking for a pair of navy blue slacks at a department store. I picked up a pair of paints and asked the clerk if he thought the pants were dress slacks or were actually more along the line of khakis.

I was there as a customer, knowing what I wanted, but not sure about the nature of the product I was looking at. I needed a second opinion from a person I had every right to believe knew more about the product line than I did. It was a situation in which that employee, having gained knowledge of the merchandise by working with it day after day, could have helped me make an informed buying decision.

But that didn't turn out to be the case. Instead, the clerk told me that he wasn't really familiar with the product line, and wasn't confident about his own knowledge of the merchandise. He told me that he thought (rather than knowing for sure) that the pants were slacks, and went on to tell me that the pants he was wearing at that moment were the same brand as the ones I was holding in my hands.

On the surface, that might have sounded like a strong recommendation, but when I looked at the pants he was wearing, I could see that they were old and rather unattractive In that case, the clerk's presence was speaking loudly, and it wasn't inspiring my confidence!

I looked at the clerk's pants and knew instantly that they weren't the pants I wanted. I thanked the young man, put the pants down, turned, and walked out of the store, on my way to another clothing store to buy a pair of slacks.

I wasn't rude to that young man, and I doubt if he even knew that it was his presence that had cost his store a sale that day. But his slacks looked as if he'd thrown them into the washer and dryer far too many times and then put them on without ironing them, which was definitely not the look I was hoping for. So I went to a competitor, who could offer me the product I was seeking.

In that example, the young man was certainly not representing the company or thinking like a doctor. He didn't fixed my problem, right there and then, by either seeking out another clerk's expert advice or by showing me another brand of pants that he knew to be slacks. But in the end, it was that clerk's presence that ultimately killed the sale, whether he ever knew it or not.

As for his employers, though they would never know about it, the store lost not only a customer that day, but they also lost the income that my purchase represented, and any real chance at my repeat business.

That's how important presence can be.

You may be thinking, "What's the big deal? It was only one pair of slacks."

But the point is: who knows how many other customers were lost that day, due to the combination of that young man's lack of product knowledge and his less than professional appearance? It's part of the hidden back door scenario we discussed earlier— and as the owner or manager of the company, you'll never see it or hear about it, you'll only see your sales numbers begin to fall. You're the doctor, so fix the problem!

In the end, what you're looking for from every one of your organization's employees is a professional appearance and a working knowledge of the company's merchandise or services. It doesn't matter what your business sells—clothing, hardware, grass seed, or anything else. Whether we're talking about a department store, a person painting houses, a fast food chain, or a doctor's office, presence is a vital key to any business success.

Looking the Part

Think about it: would you have confidence in your doctor if you walked into the office and saw that he looked as if he'd been out all night, but told you that he needed to perform some type of major surgery on you—right then and there? No, you'd probably be diplomatic about it, but you'd tell him, as kindly as possible, that you'd like to have a little time to think it over. Then you'd immediately go out and seek a second opinion, preferably from someone who was able to present a more professional image and approach to your situation.

It works the exact same in any other customer service industry—first impressions matter a great deal, and there's no getting around that simple, inescapable fact. When a company representative looks polished, regardless of their position, that person gives customers the impression that since they look professional, they're also likely to possess expert knowledge about their company's product line. Sometimes, that professional first impression alone is enough to make a customer feel comfortable enough to trust, work with, and take advice from that company representative, which is more than half the battle!

The other half of the battle is getting your employees to care about your customers and about the company as a whole as if they were the own—but we'll talk more about how to do that in upcoming chapters. In this chapter, we're concentrating on the importance of creating favorable first impressions with your clients.

The important thing for you, as a manager, supervisor, or company owner, is to make sure that all of the people in your organization who deal with customers present a totally professional image and a superior knowledge of your product line at all times. In other words, they need to both look and act the part of the professionals they are.

Now, that doesn't mean that every employee has to know every answer to every conceivable question a customer might ask—that would be unreasonable But it does mean that they must be willing to seek out the answers when a customer presents them with something they're unfamiliar with—just as a doctor seeks out a specialist to help when they are faced with a situation that is beyond their field of expertise.

Going back to my previous example of shopping for a pair of pants, the young man who helped me could have easily acknowledged that he wasn't sure of the difference between the two choices I'd given him. Then it would have been perfectly logical for him to have sought out a more experienced clerk for advice I would have admired his resourcefulness, and I might have then looked at another line of merchandise—and possibly might have even bought a pair of slacks before I left the store.

But we'll never know if that would have been the case, because the clerk didn't do any of those things. So I walked out of the store without making a purchase, shaking my head at the young man's lack of professionalism—and at the overall lack of professionalism the entire store had exhibited by allowing that clerk to wait on customers in such an unprofessional manner.

It was a shame, but that sort of situation happens millions of times in millions of business places throughout the world every single day.

Presence—it's so important.

But let me end this chapter by saying that the process of improving customer service is most effectively accomplished by taking it step by step, getting everyone in the organization involved, from top to bottom. That way, every member of the team will have the opportunity to feel as if their contribution is important to the overall success of the project—because it is.

By paying close attention to every part of the customer service improvement process, you'll also be able to keep your employees from becoming overwhelmed. So, instead of making giant, sweeping changes all at once, you'll accomplish more by making incremental changes that will allow employees to enjoy the process as it unfolds.

The Best Time Is Right Now

Providing superior customer service is the lifeblood of any company, regardless of what field that company may be in, and you simply can't afford to present an image to your customer that's less than first-rate. If you don't present that professional image, you can be assured that your competition will—and your customers will begin taking their business elsewhere!

So give some genuine thought to how important a professional presence can be to your company's overall success. Your decision could mark the beginning—or the eventual end—for you and your company, if you don't begin immediately to upgrade your professional image!

In every field of business, consumers are looking for great customer service, and for a great many clients, customer service is actually more important than price! In fact, the overwhelming majority of consumers rate superior customer service as the number one factor in their decision to return to a given business the next time they have a need for that particular product or service.

So, what would happen if you instituted a program that would turn your company into a place of great customer service instead of just good customer service, beginning with establishing a strong professional presence when customers entered your place of business? How much more business do you think you could generate if everything every member of your company said and did reinforced an image of true professionalism in the customer's mind? And how many times do you think those customers would return to buy your product or service over the course of a lifetime, if they truly believed that your company was tops when it came to superior customer service?

Remember, repeat business is like having customers hand you free money! You didn't have to spend thousands or millions of dollars to lure them into buying your product or service. They're already convinced that they'll be continuing to buy from you from this point on.

But the choice is yours. I'm hoping that you'll choose to open your company's doors and let all of those eager customers flock inside!

Again, don't put it off.

Every day that you fail to begin improving your company's customer service will cost you—indefinitely—both in lost new business (like the example of my shopping for slacks) and in the all-important realm of repeat business.

So start now! The sooner you begin providing superior customer service, the sooner you'll find customers standing in line, just waiting to bring new business—and repeat business—into your organization.

7

One Customer or Employee at a Time

Keeping the Doctor concept in mind, let's take a few moments to scrub up, just as a doctor would. Clear your thoughts and open your mind to what's about to come next. Your half way through the book at this point and I'm hoping that learning to think like a doctor is becoming a habit for you. That way, you'll easily be able to pass those thought patterns on to your employees, who will then begin to feel empowered to take increasingly better care of your customers It's a concept that works—I know from personal experience.

While you're scrubbing up, give some thought to how much one person can impact your company's image and bottom line. Each interaction between a customer or employee represents an opportunity to create a positive experience—one that will reflect favorably upon the entire company. As a doctor, it's not prudent to rush a decision or diagnosis. It's always better to take a little time, give the matter some genuine thought, and then to act upon the best plan possible. After all, if a doctor makes a rush decision, the results could prove to be fatal for the patient—and the same basic theory applies to the decisions you make concerning your organization's customer service policies.

Once you're settled, relaxed, and open, let's move on.

Service or Disservice?

In this chapter, we're going to talk about how to deal effectively with one customer or employee at a time, just as you would like a doctor to do with you. Can you image your doctor telling you, in the middle of surgery, that they needed to run over to the next room and work on another patient who was also undergoing surgery? That sounds crazy, right? But that's exactly what you and your employees are doing on a daily basis.

In order to give great customer service, it's important that you work with only one customer, employee, or issue at a time. That may sound simple, but in most cases, that's not what happens. For instance, how often have you found yourself working with an issue, employee, or customer, only to be interrupted by something else or some other person? In a heartbeat, you've quickly excused yourself and you're off to attend to that interruption.

Even if you leave the issue, customer, or employee only briefly, when you return, you'll be working on two things at once, whether you realize it or not. You may think you're physically working with only one issue at a time, but your mind is actually working on both at some level.

When that happens, it really boils down to giving only half of your efforts to each of the situations involved, which is unacceptable if you're truly intent on offering your clients superior customer service. When in comes to your customers, each one of them deserves 100% of your attention while you're working with them—until the situation is resolved to everyone's satisfaction That's a vitally important concept for everyone in your organization to understand.

It would be nice if we could just round up all our customers and employees and take care of all of their needs, issues, and concerns at one time, but that's not possible. Instead, we must focus on each of our customers or employees as if they were the only ones we had, because every one of them is valuable to our company's bottom line.

It's important to include employees in the overall equation, because they're the ones who will be working with your customers, and if you want your customers to keep coming back, they must be well treated. Begin the process by letting every employee know their efforts are appreciated, and they'll pass that attitude on to your customers. So slow down and take the time to work with each employee, one at a time, and let them know that they're a valuable part of your organization's success, which is why you trust them to be totally accountable for their actions.

That process begins with keeping yourself in the here and now. Be present, moment to moment, living today for its own sake and leaving tomorrow until it comes. Most of us have calendars that are filled with things to do and people to see, and that's fine, but no matter how busy your calendar is, business success still boils down to just one customer, employee, or issue at a time, and devoting your entire energy to that moment.

Have you every tried to read a book all at once? It can't be done. Each page of that book must be read, one at a time, until you've completed the book The same is true with your appointment book. You can't take care of the entire book at the same time. In order to build your business and to succeed as a leader, you must take each item in your day book and move forward to the next—only after each preceding issue has been fully resolved.

True Leaders

If you stay on top of the day-to-day business, all of your items will get taken care of eventually—in fact, if you break the word "eventually" down, the term means that things get done event by event, one event at a time That's what great customer service is all about, and if you can instill that concept in every one of your employees, your organization will take a giant step toward success. Your percentage of satisfied customers will increase, your repeat business will skyrocket, and your happy customers will provide you with the best type of advertising— positive word of mouth.

Think of it as a doctor would. You can't treat every patient at the same time or with the same methods. Every one of your patients has different needs, and you must carefully tune in to what they're saying if you're going to prescribe an appropriate remedy for their unique situation.

In your position as a leader, you'll be dealing with lots of projects, even when you begin to address them one at a time. After all, having lots of business is the only way for an organization to be successful. Therefore, it's important to take time between your various tasks to regroup between them. Stop and have a cup of coffee, go meet with some of your customers or employees, and then move on to the next issue on your list with a clear mind. Learning how to take the time needed to complete one task, relax, refocus, and then move on to the next task will make you a more efficient leader, and will reduce your stress level considerably.

But there are also other benefits to your organization when you walk around and interact with employees or customers. First, it helps you take your mind off the previous problem by focusing on something else that isn't as pressing or stressful Second, it helps your employees and customers see you when you're not stressed and uptight, which, in turn, helps lower their own stress levels. Third, it raises the morale of the entire organization to know that the boss has a genuine interest in every employee, customer, and the company as a whole.

The key is not to get overwhelmed and then to give up after you've just dealt with a difficult client or situation. While you're taking take the time to stop and refocus your energy, you'll be able to get better acquainted with your company, employees, and customers, which can never be a bad thing. Each time you deal with another human being, whether it's a customer, CEO, or the person who sweeps the floors, approaching them honestly and openly will make a world of difference to everyone involved.

Every time you reach out from your heart and take the time to honestly understand a customer or employee, the overall openness and trust level increases, and your ability to satisfy your clients improves. Removing yourself from the center of the situation and placing the emphasis on the other person is really what great customer service is all about. Your goal will be to help the other person accomplish their goals, which will, in turn, bring you closer to your own goals. Every employee in your organization should understand this concept completely.

The customer's needs come first—period.

It might help to think of it this way. You go to your doctor with a sore arm. But just as you begin to describe your symptoms, the doctor interrupts you and says, "You think you've got a sore arm? I'll tell you, I sprained mine playing golf yesterday, and it hurts like you wouldn't believe!"

Your confidence level in that doctor would instantly go down, because it would be obvious that the doctor's first concern was for themselves, and not for you. You might even get angry, since you came in for help and advice, but the focus of the conversation had immediately turned to the doctor's problems, and not yours.

That's how your customers feel when they come to your organization for help and advice. They don't care about your company's problems—they only want help with their own. They look to you to be the doctor and to provide an appropriate remedy—and they have every right to expect that you'll come up with a solution to their needs and concerns. They expect you to be accountable for helping them, and they'll hold you accountable for the outcome, whether that outcome is satisfactory or not.

As a leader, modeling a caring, responsible, honest, and open attitude for your employees encourages them to do the same with your customers. They'll learn how to talk with clients in an open, friendly manner, and then to assist them with all of their needs, insuring that every customer walks away totally satisfied—just as they would if they'd been visiting their local doctor's office with an ailment of some sort.

Unless you stop and gather information—by asking appropriate questions and then listening to the answers—you can't get a feel for what your customer is going through. Without gaining the proper background information, you also can't know how the problem came about, how it's currently affecting the customer, or what steps you can take to remedy the situation. The only effective way to do that is to keep the customer's needs in center focus at all times.

As the leader of your organization, instilling a doctor's mentality and attitude in every employee begins with you. Let your people know you care about them, and they'll begin to care about others. Caring creates more caring, but it doesn't happen by magic—your employees will ultimately take their cues from you!

The Answer is Clear

You're the doctor, so fix the problem—and train your employees to think like doctors, too. If every employee in your company developed that mentality, everyone's trust level would go up, the entire workplace would become a more pleasant environment, and the good feelings of the employees would be passed along to your customers. Good feelings breed more good feelings, so create an environment in which everyone feels good about what they're doing within the company and about what they're able to do for the customer.

But in order for it all to work, the good feelings must start at the top and work their way throughout your organization. It's a ripple effect, and once it begins, you'll be amazed at the results. You'll begin to see better managers, better employees, and an improved bottom line—without having to change any personnel! Suddenly, even those employees whose attitude wasn't good at the start of the program will begin to show more concern for their relationships with fellow employees, the company, and most importantly, about offering your customers superior customer service!

It all begins with your attitude, and a great attitude is contagious. Compassion, honesty, and openness are infectious—

your employees will respond. Your organization can improve its bottom line, attract new business, and continue to enjoy repeat business, but it all starts with you, and how you teach your employees to treat themselves and your organization's customers—one at a time.

8

Let's Keep it Simple

As always, we'll begin this chapter by taking a moment to scrub up, getting our thoughts together, clearing our heads, and opening our minds to what the material that's about to be presented. After all, what's past is past, and we need to let it go, so that it doesn't affect our thoughts or attitudes about next situation we're going to discuss, just as any good doctor would do.

There's an old adage that's as true today as it ever was, which says, "start with the simplest solution, whether the problem is major or minor, before moving on to a more complex solution." What you're about to read may seem too simple, but that's the exact point I'm trying to make, and represents a good way of interacting with all of your customers and employees.

So take a few moments, breathe deeply, and let all of your previous problems go. Just relax, open your heart and mind to the possibilities you're about to discover, and when you're ready, continue reading.

Simple and Easy

Every customer who visits your company has needs and questions they want answered or problems they want solved—otherwise, they wouldn't have sought you out in the first place. And every need, question or problem represents an opportunity for you to provide your clients with superior customer service, and for making each customer's experience at your place of business as pleasant as possible.

But what do we mean when we suggest keeping it simple while dealing with customers and employees, when some of their issues are anything but simple? As we work our way through this chapter, one of the key factors to keep in mind, as we've said in previous chapters, is that the change in your policies and attitudes may take some time—so make them step by step. Your organization's commitment to great customer service is for the long haul, so you don't have to be in a hurry to do everything all at once. When someone commits to a long-term investment, the foundation of that investment needs to be solid. So take the time to do it right, which begins by keeping things simple.

Begin the process by looking at yourself. Are you cool-headed, or do you usually get too wound up in your various projects? If you're like many business people, you get an idea in your head that something needs to be done, such as starting a new project or improving an existing one, and you become so involved with it, that it begins to consume all of your time and energy.

I'm no stranger to that phenomenon myself, and I learned some important lessons about keeping things simple during the creation of this book. Not long after starting the book project, my stress level went right through the roof. Luckily for me, I had some excellent advisors who constantly kept reminding me to slow down, take a deep breath, and think about the overall project in its simplest terms Creating a book wasn't rocket science, they said, and the world wouldn't end if I didn't get everything accomplished in one day—in fact, it wasn't possible to do that. A book project is a relatively long process, involving a number of steps, and if I just concentrated on getting each step done, one by one, I could break the seemingly overwhelming project into smaller, more manageable steps, and would ultimately produce a book I could be proud of.

So I can tell you from my own personal experience: take it easy, and keep it simple Then, once you've adopted that attitude in your own business and personal life, you can begin to encourage your employees to do the same. Once that happens, you'll find that the stress level in your organization will go down, morale will improve, and productivity will go up—all three of which are worthwhile results.

Another piece of advice: if you find that you can't seem to slow down and simplify, don't beat yourself up about it. Remember that old habits die hard, and before you can bring a new philosophy into your life, you have to clear out your old beliefs and attitudes.

You're the doctor, so fix the problem!

If you were remodeling a room, you'd have a plan in place for what the new room was going to look like, even before you began. But that plan wouldn't involve leaving all the old furniture in place while also bringing in the new furniture. Before the new stuff could be put into the room, you'd first have to get rid of the old stuff.

But even if you wanted to, there's no way that you could take all the old furniture out at the same time. You'd have to pick up each piece of furniture, one at a time, and carry them out.

There may be pieces of the old furniture that work well for you, and you'll want to save them for reuse in your new modeling scheme. That's fine, but you'll still need to take them out of the room before you begin your total remodel—and it still can only be done one piece at a time.

Then, once everything is out of the room, you finish the cleanup process by sweeping up all the dust from the floor and vacuuming the cobwebs from the ceiling. Then, and only then, are you ready to start bringing in the new furniture—but you can only bring in that furniture one piece at a time. The entire process can only be done step by step.

So if it seems to be taking an inordinate amount of time for you to make the transition, just remind yourself that you're in the midst of remodeling, and it's a process of cleaning out the old to make room for the new. That will take some of the pressure off. Even amid the dust of remodeling, you have a vision of what your new room is going to look like when it's complete—but like everything else in this world, remodeling your attitude is a step by step process.

Avoiding Unnecessary Stress

Each new project comes with its own challenges, things to do, and people to see, and before long, stress can begin to set in. When that happens to the person at the top, which would be you, stress spreads like a virus, and soon everyone begins to feel it— your employees, your family, and ultimately, your customers.

Yes, even your customers will begin to feel it when your stress level begins to increase, and it will adversely affect your bottom line. So make incremental steps when you begin the process of improving your organization's customer service Then, whenever it feels as if it's not coming along fast enough or not looking exactly the way you originally envisioned it, remember that you're in the process of remodeling, and hurrying the job won't help.

The transition should be a smooth as possible for everyone concerned, but it begins with you. When it comes to making major changes within an organization, especially those involving customer service, the key to making those changes successfully begins with the person who implemented those changes in the first place—the person at the top.

As always, the best way to lead is by example, and in this case, keeping an even keel is crucial to the successful implementation of your improved customer service program That begins by helping your employees learn to simplify their projects by dealing with them on a step by step basis.

No Surprises—Keep Everyone Involved

The first step toward great customer service is to make sure that everyone involved in a project, understands the project's goals. Many times, I've seen a good project passed down from upper management without letting their people know everything about it—which is always a formula for disaster. With each new person who gets involved without being properly briefed on such things as goals, time frame, cost, and all the other factors that make up a project, the chances for problems increase exponentially. Every project starts off as a great idea, but as more and more people become stressed from not fully understanding the project, the project quickly becomes more difficult for everyone involved. The stress level increases, enthusiasm for the project goes down, and eventually the whole project becomes a tedious burden for everyone involved—including the customer.

When a project has degenerated to that point, human nature kicks in and people begin to point fingers at each other, blaming each other for delays and frustrations, instead of working together to accomplish a common goal. That's where the concept of standing firm with accountability comes in, as we discussed in a previous chapter. Everyone, from top to bottom of the organization, needs to be accountable for their part of the project. If everyone is accountable, they'll take it upon themselves to understand the project thoroughly, and will work to do their part to bring that project to completion.

If I had to summarize the basic concept of this book in just one word, that word would be accountability, because it's the key factor in offering superior customer service. In fact, without accountability, there can be no real customer service, because no one would care enough to take responsibility for making sure every customer was totally satisfied. Without accountability, any customer service that took place would be completely accidental!

As a leader in your organization, you want to model respect, both for your customers and employees. Your employees will follow your lead as long as they feel as if they're being treated with respect and are being fully briefed on what you're trying to achieve. Keeping all employees informed will make them feel like a part of the process—and as if they're a part of a team, seeking answers to customer concerns and issues.

There's no need to implement your new, improved customer service program with a heavy hand. All it really involves is beginning to hold each and every employee truly accountable! Since you're in business for the long haul, putting customer service should be at the very top of your list of projects to be done, because without customers, you have no business! So begin today to implement your new program, although you don't have to do it all at once. Your goal is to make each employee accountable—beginning with yourself!

Putting it All into Action

The first step, since you're the doctor, is to slow down, relax, and while you're scrubbing up and getting ready for your next project, clear your mind of what took place in the past, since it has no bearing on what is about to come, and begin to open yourself to the opportunities that lie ahead.

Then, when you're ready to move forward, keep these two words foremost in your mind: accountability and simplicity. It's easy to be accountable for everything you do, as long as you continue to be accountable from one moment to the next, because as a wise person once said, "our lives are made up of an endless series of moments." If you are accountable for each moment, every day, you'll ultimately have been accountable for an entire lifetime.

Accountability is dependent on staying involved. As long as each person continues to be involved, they have to be accountable, by definition. Problems really begin when someone "washes their hands" of a project, signifying that they longer consider themselves accountable for what happens from that point on. But if everyone stays involved and takes responsibility for their part in the process, your projects will run much more smoothly, from start to finish. That doesn't mean there won't be difficulties along the way, of course, but people who are accountable for their role in a project will be much more likely to seek solutions to problems quickly and efficiently.

As a leader, you'll need to reprogram your own habits in a significant way First, you'll need to take time out of your busy schedule at least three times a month (although it would be more effective if it were done every day) to follow up on each project, just to see how it's coming along and to make sure that every employee is continuing to keep it simple by staying accountable for their particular phase of the project.

Simplicity and accountability are intertwined, and are key factors to developing and maintaining great customer service. Teach your employees to think like doctors, and when they see something that needs attention, empower them to fix the problem!

Keeping on top of projects by staying involved greatly reduces the possibility of problems that might get so far out of hand that they can't be fixed on the spot It might help to think of problems as if they were fires. A small fire tends to get bigger if it's not extinguished right away. But even if the fire eventually burns itself out, there will still be a scorched place where that fire had been That scorched place could represent your customer—and if you let your customer get burned badly enough, they may never return.

So make sure that all of your employees feel as if they have the power to put out fires—or better yet, to prevent fires altogether, if it appears that a fire might be a possibility. If you work diligently to protect your customers, they're going to sense that, and if your customers feel as if you're always looking out for their welfare, you'll be well on your way toward providing the type of customer service that builds loyalty and increased business.

In today's competitive marketplace, every company must find a way to get an edge on the competition, and one of the most effective ways to gain such an edge is by providing superior customer service. Remember, if you don't act on this concept as soon as possible, your competition will, because consumers are constantly looking for great customer service, and are even willing to pay a bit more when they find it. Customer service is the key to repeat business, and also to creating that intangible, but very real and enormously effective type of advertising—positive word of mouth.

Make no mistake: just having good customer service is no longer enough. It's time for you to transform your company into a place that offers great customer service! It will boost morale, reduce stress, increase customer loyalty, and improve your bottom line, so start building great customer service now! You have everything to gain, and absolutely nothing to lose. Open the door and let your new customers in! They'll begin flocking to your company because they'll know that every single person in your organization is accountable for their actions at all times.

There's no doubt about it. It's a win-win situation, and one that's completely within your power to accomplish—if you simply take it one step at a time!

9

Step by Step

In this chapter, we're going to focus on how to improve your company's customer service, one step at a time—even if those steps happen to be baby steps. The information will go hand-in-hand with the previous chapter, but it's important enough that I want to emphasize it separately.

But before we get into our new discussion, let's take some time to scrub up and get ready for our next set of information. Let your mind relax, calm your thoughts, and let's get away from whatever may have been on your mind before, because none of that has any relevance at this moment. Take a deep breath, open your mind, and give some thought to this question: How would the concept of keeping it simple be able to help both you and your staff slow down and begin to give each of your customers the amount of time that would be necessary to satisfy each issue before moving on to the next one? When you're ready, let's begin talking about exactly how to provide that sort of superior customer service, step by step.

Moving Forward with an Open Mind

I can't overstress how important it is to keep all of the employees who are working on a particular project involved in the process at all times. Keeping them truly involved creates genuine accountability without having them become over-whelmed.

First, let me talk briefly about my own experience as a manager, and how the typical manager feels when a new project is announced by the CEO or someone from upper management In most cases, the project is announced by a memo, sent out to all the various division managers, telling them there'll be a meeting about the project—one that all managers must attend.

The first thing that comes to the minds of those managers is, "Oh boy, what is it now? Even more work for me to do? As if I don't have enough to do already!"

That sort of attitude is reflective of the workload that faces most middle management people. It doesn't mean they're lazy—it just means that they have quite a bit of day-to-day responsibilities already. They may have been feeling overwhelmed even before the memo arrived on their desks, and they instantly begin to worry about how they're going to take even more time out of their busy schedules to take on a new project.

But if you're a typical company head, and the one who issued the memo in the first place, I can assure you that you're not going to hear any of that. The vast majority of managers aren't going to speak their minds and tell you how they really feel about adding another major project to their workload, but I promise, the feelings will be there.

That type of scenario is exactly what we're hoping to avoid in this chapter We want to protect your employees from the fear and anger associated with being overwhelmed and overworked —and it can be done, but like all of the concepts we've discussed so far, the process has to start at the top.

Don't get me wrong. I'm not trying to tell you how to run your company, but I will be telling you how I've seen it work best in the past, from my own personal experience, and if you listen with the open mind, as we always talk about at the beginning of each chapter, I'm hoping that you'll see the wisdom of what I'm saying. It will help you create a team spirit among your employees, and when that team spirit has caught on throughout your organization, employees will be eager to do the best for everyone involved. Once everyone begins thinking and acting like a team, it will mark the beginning of your company's quest for providing great customer service.

As the person issuing the memo, it would benefit you to think like the doctor you are, preparing to go into major surgery. Long before you issued the memo and scheduled the mandatory managers' meeting, you studied the upcoming project thoroughly and from all angles. You considered the ins and outs of the project, and have a good handle on what it will entail. You've talked with the client at length, and you know exactly what they want, what the expected outcome will be, and how the project will affect your company. You know the time frame involved, the budget, and all of the hundreds of little details that will need to be addressed to successfully complete the project.

Only when you can say that you've carefully considered every aspect of the project will you finally be ready to send out the memo and schedule the meeting. From my own years of experience, I can tell you that if there's any aspect of the project about which you still have questions, you're not ready to send the memo or set up the meeting. As a true leader, it's your responsibility to hold yourself accountable for being able to tell your managers exactly what they're going to be signing up for.

All Feedback is Useful

Once you're completely prepared, informed, and ready, you can call your meeting But in that meeting, you'll still need to be open to each manager's feedback after you have given them all the information you've gathered It's a crucial step, so let them talk, one manager at a time, offering their own unique perspectives on the project and the role of their department in getting it completed.

In your meeting, let everyone know exactly what your thinking is, including why adding this particular project to the company at this particular time is important, and also explaining why superior customer service will be crucial to its successful completion. Letting everyone know exactly what your thoughts and feelings are will cut back on the surprise factor, and will give your the managers time to absorb the information and its importance to the company as a whole, and not just to their individual departments.

Offering a thorough explanation of the project and its importance to the company will also make your managers feel as if they're a valued member of your team—which they are. Once you've begun the feedback process, allowing your managers to offer genuine input and insights will not only further reinforce the team member concept, but it will allow you to hear about some aspects of the project that you may not have considered until that point.

As the leader of an organization, you'll probably have to bite your lip at various times during the feedback process, but it's vital that you fight the urge to defend your original point of view and genuinely listen to the thoughts and feelings of your management team. After all, they're "in the trenches" daily, and they'll have insights that may be slightly different from your own—especially if you haven't been following the advice I gave earlier about spending quality time with your customers and employees on a regular basis. (If you haven't been doing that, you might want to take some time to thumb back several chapters, and reread those parts!)

The point is: you're not giving up your control of the decision-making process when you listen to other team members voice their thoughts and concerns about a new project. The fact is, you never know were the next great idea is going to come from, and if you've followed my advice on making everyone in your organization totally accountable, you can be assured that whatever suggestions they offer will be for the good of everyone concerned. In the end, interacting with other accountable people is the best way to keep yourself accountable, as well.

Always remember: this isn't a short-term concept—it's meant to provide a lifetime improvement for yourself and for your organization. So take it step by step, and even if you have to take baby steps, it's better than falling down!

Bringing it All Together

After your meeting with your management team, send them out to have a similar meeting with their own people. Have them explain every aspect of the project to their people, just as you did for them. Then have them ask their people for their insights and concerns, just as you did. That way, everyone from top to bottom will be informed of the project and its importance, and everyone will have had the chance to add their own input, which will further enhance the feeling of team spirit throughout the organization.

Finally, hold a third meeting, this time devoting most of the time to allowing the various managers report the concerns and insights they gathered from their people. Again, many of these insights will be very valuable, because they'll address things that might not have occurred to you during your initial information gathering process, regardless of how thorough you tried to be.

Don't get defensive! Remember, these are your team members, offering their thoughts on how to achieve victory, using their own unique knowledge of the various aspects of your company's day-to-day operations.

It's important that all three meetings be stress-free—and creating a team spirit within your organization will reduce the stress level to a significant degree, because everyone will be approaching the project from a "let's all work together to gain a victory" perspective, rather than having the entire project feel like just another added burden or struggle.

At the end of the third meeting, thank all of your managers for their time, energy, insights, and cooperation, and encourage them to have a brief meeting with their own people, just to express your thanks to everyone on the team. Then reemphasize your belief that each employee will be held accountable for whatever aspect of the project they've been assigned, from beginning to end—not as a threat, but as a gesture of respect for them as a valued member of the team.

Making your people feel like an important part of the overall process is a critical factor in becoming successful as a company. Thinking as a doctor, you've given your patient's surgery a great deal of thought and study. Then, just as a skilled surgeon would do, you've gathered together a team of competent aides who are totally accountable for doing their best to make the overall operation a success. You know you can count on them to do as they promise, and you, being totally accountable for your own aspect of the operation and respecting the integrity and skill of your associates, will be able to guarantee your patient the outcome they desire—on time and on budget.

As head surgeon, you're responsible for overseeing all the aspects of the operation as it's taking place, always trusting your people's continued commitment to full accountability. You'll keep an eye out for complications, and address them quickly as soon as they occur. You'll make sure your associates are also staying on top of their own responsibilities, and are holding their own people fully accountable throughout the process. You'll hold regular meetings, both with your staff and with your customers, to make sure that everything is proceeding smoothly—and if everyone continues to remain accountable, those meetings won't need to be as long, since all you'll be doing is getting updates on the project's progress.

Finally, when the project has been completed, you won't just send the patient/customers back out into the world. But as a good doctor would do, you'll ask the customers to check back with you after a period of time, just to let you know how it all worked out. If you haven't heard from your customers after that period, you'll then take responsibility and give them a call or written letter.

In Summary

Remember that superior customer service is based on meaningful, honest interaction between everyone involved, and creating a climate for that type of interaction can only be accomplished by keeping it simple, taking the process on a step by step basis Hold yourself and your managers totally accountable, and have your managers hold their people accountable, as well. Expecting people to be accountable is actually a sign of respect, and you'll be pleasantly surprised to see how people will respond when they know they're being treated with genuine respect They become happy to be a part of the team, and will do more than they have ever done to help the team accomplish its goals.

Surround yourself with the best surgical team you can, and once that team has been assembled, never miss an opportunity to let them know how much you appreciate them—you'll be amazed at the results!

10

Your Money

Whether you're self-employed, working for someone else, or just want to improve your own self-worth, this chapter will set you on the right path. And if you're a CEO or a manager, we're going to talk about what you must do every day in order to stay on top of the customer service game—and well above your competition. Being Number 1—that's your goal!

But as always, before we move forward with this chapter, you'll need to scrub up. Take a few moments to get centered, relax your mind, and open yourself to life's possibilities. Nothing that has transpired before is important at this moment. The only thing that matters is for you to become open and to get ready for the information that is about to come. Clear your mind of the old and open yourself to the new.

Once you're scrubbed up, let me talk briefly about the importance of doing your own scrubbing up and then passing the concept on to your employees. Having your people begin to think like doctors will add a sense of importance, dignity, and self-worth to all of their endeavors. Of course, you won't generally be dealing with life-and-death situations, but the truth is that most of the issues and concerns doctors see aren't life-threatening, either. But their decisions do affect the lives of their patients, and so do the decisions made by your customers and employees. Have your employees try to center and refocus between patients/customers, and you'll soon begin to see a positive change in the way your employees treat both their customers and their co-workers.

The Truth of the Matter

Perhaps the title of this chapter seems incongruous. Why would we be talking about your money, when we've been talking about great customer service? Well, if your first thought when reading those words was about your own personal money, we're off to a bad start, because in order to properly view customer service, everyone involved—from top to bottom—must be thinking like a member of a team. After all, no one person can run a company. It takes a team—a good, strong, unified team of talented and dedicated individuals—to make a company run well.

With that team concept in mind, take a moment to think about what kind of a team you would have gathered around you if you lived in a perfect world. How would that team look? How would they speak? How would they act? Most importantly, how would they treat your customers—and how would your customers respond to such a team?

Some of these questions can be answered easily, but the real challenges begin when we have to come out of our perfect world and return to reality. But having seen what a perfect team would look like, it's time to ask yourself how you can get as close as possible to creating your dream team—right now, right where you are.

Remember, this is your money, and you control who works for you and your customers. But there are lots of other considerations, as well, beginning with the old adage: "you get exactly what you pay for."

How many professional teams wallow in the lower division of their league because they either can't or won't pay the price to bring in the most talented players? Sure, every now and then, a team with a limited budget will come out of nowhere and win a championship—but for the most part; it's the teams that put out the money necessary to attract quality players that dominate their sport.

From my own 25 years of experience in the customer service industry, from top to bottom, I've learned that when you hold on to your dollars too tightly and don't put out the money necessary to bring in top-quality people, your entire organization begins to suffer. When you don't offer attractive employment packages, you begin to attract employees who don't care about your business or customers. They're only there for a paycheck, and there's no company loyalty because it's obvious that the company doesn't care about them! That's a formula for disaster, and one to be avoided, at all costs.

On the other hand, you could loosen the purse strings and begin to attract talented, motivated, loyal employees—ones who enjoy an above-average quality of life and think of themselves as valued members of a winning team. Now, when I say "above-average," that doesn't mean they're outrageously overpaid For most working people, simply making another one or two dollars an hour can make a significant difference in their ability to provide for their families and will build loyalty toward their employer. If your pay scale is slightly above that of the competition, you'll greatly reduce the chance of losing valuable employees, as well, because they'll have less incentive to leave for greener pastures.

Of course, you won't be able to hold on to every employee forever, but paying them a dollar or two above the industry standard should keep those employees with you for several extra years, at the very least. Keeping your employees happy is vital for keeping your customers happy and for building repeat business. It's like an insurance policy that will pay big dividends over time—which is the way you should be looking at it, because you're in business for the long haul.

Always remember: you're the doctor, so fix the problem!

Practicing Thinking Like a Doctor

For a moment, let's look at skimping on money, using a doctor's office scenario as an example. You walk into the office and you're greeted by a receptionist with a cold and uncaring attitude. You look around and see that she's surrounded by office equipment that's old and outdated. What would be your first impression of that office?

After checking in, you walk over to a set of beat-up chairs, some of which have tears in the fabric, and sit down. You pick up a magazine that's ten years old and start to thumb through it. But what impression has all this made? The chances are you're not going to be filled with confidence about the doctor or his staff. You'll wonder if perhaps the doctor isn't prosperous enough to be able to afford new equipment for the receptionist or new furniture for the waiting room. Maybe there will even be some doubt in your mind as to whether the doctor is competent to practice medicine in the first place. It may not make sense, but when you look around and see that everything's rundown, your mind can't help but wonder if this is really the place to seek help for your problem.

Well, those exact same thought processes go on in the minds of customers who enter your place of business. Have you brought your business establishment's appearance up to par? Does your company give off an air of prosperity when a customer walks in? Does your staff appear competent and happy to be there? Are they nicely groomed and exhibiting a friendly, caring attitude to every customer they greet? All of these factors come into play when your customer walks through the front door of your place of business.

The Big Picture

To gain some perspective on how it's supposed to be, let's go back in time for a few moments, and get back to basics. From my research, and from talking to many customers and employees of all ages over the years, something I continually hear is a longing for customer service—the way it used to be.

Of course, we can't physically go back in time, but there's no reason why we can't create the type of excellent working environment that existed in many companies back in the 60s and 70s. Those decades were, for the most part, very good years for most working class folks, and were also profitable periods for most companies at the same time. Working conditions were good, companies took care of their employees, both while they worked for the company and after they retired, and all of that good naturally translated to excellence in taking care of customers. Even though times have changed, and there are some things that can't be changed back, the key factors remain. Taking good care of your employees allows them to take good care of your customers.

Since we're talking about your money and your customers, let's move a step further and look at what your customers are really looking for, since your customers are the essential part in determining whether your company makes money or not. When customers are looking for help to solve their issues, they're seeking someone who can meet a specific need or desire. But they're also seeking something beyond that, as well, whether consciously or unconsciously Customers are also seeking someone who really cares about their concerns. They want to find someone who can act as both a counselor and a friend.

They also want someone who will respond to their needs without being judgmental and will maintain their confidentiality. For example, whether customers are looking for a hair transplant or simply trying to fit into an outfit that's slightly too small, they want to know that their integrity is going to be respected and maintained.

Perhaps that's as good a definition of superior customer service as we could find, and it's the kind of thing that enters a customer's mind whenever they walk into a place of business. Just think about the places where you shop most often. How has your average experience been while doing business there? If you've been back there a number of times, the chances are good that you found the overall experience pleasurable and the attitude of the staff friendly and caring. They made you feel special, and made it clear that they were happy to have you visit. The place of business looked prosperous and up-to-date, and the employees were well informed and knowledgeable about their product line. If you were in a department store, someone was nearby to assist you without your having to hunt someone down. All of these factors were important to you as a customer, and the same thing is true of the customers who visit your place of business every day.

For many years, I've been working hands-on with my customers, helping them see their options and solving their problems, because I know that both of those factors are what keeps them coming back to see me again. Addressing customer concerns and issues should always be your top priority, because if you don't, there will be a competitor who will provide the type of customer service that every customer has the right to expect. Of course, there are some customers who are just looking for low prices, but when something goes wrong, they quickly change their thinking, and they'll be a little more discriminating when it comes to making their next purchase, having learned the value of superior customer service.

Working on New Key Factors

Playing the price war game can only go so far in creating a successful business. In order to stay in business for the long term, which should always be your goal, you must add a superior customer service component to your arsenal of weapons. Low prices aren't enough by themselves. Consumers expect reasonable prices, of course, and will generally shop around for a competitive price. But once their choice comes down to a couple establishments that are close in price, they'll look next at what type of customer service those companies offer. So don't delay implementing your own company's customer service improvements—it's an edge that's relatively easy to gain, but it can pay huge dividends in customer satisfaction, employee morale, and increased profits.

Achieving customer service excellence is something that really takes no great time expenditure It simply takes proper training and an insistence on complete accountability, from top to bottom.

My own years of experience have taken me to some very large and well-known companies, including some upscale companies that you'd think would be offering nothing but top-notch customer service. Unfortunately, some of those businesses only offer that top-notch service to their biggest clients, which can be a deadly mistake, because word of mouth (that old nemesis we've talked about many times) gets around, and those customers who aren't getting special treatment will begin to feel slighted—as well they should. Superior customer service can't be a hit-and-miss affair—it's got to be a total commitment, across the board.

Customer service excellence begins by educating everyone in the organization about your product line. The more everyone knows about the product, the better, because they can then use that knowledge to educate your customers. When a customer comes into your establishment, they want information, and they want to feel a sense of confidence in the salespeople conveying that information. They want quick, solid, well-informed answers to their questions, and they'll buy from the person they feel actually cares about them and their needs.

That doesn't mean a salesperson has to have an advanced degree or special certification to help a customer. It does mean that your company should focus on educating your salespeople thoroughly about every item in your product line. If that means absorbing only small bits of information at a time, that's fine. No one learns how to walk without having to take a few baby steps—remember, this is a process, and it won't happen all at once!

For instance, take an employee of a fast food restaurant. The first day, they learn as much as they can about hamburger, and the second day, they learn about fries. It's important to try to keep the process as simple and fun as possible. There's no need to stress a new employee out on the first or second day. If the manager does create too much stress, that stress will be conveyed to the customers, and may lead to having the new employee quit—both of which are undesirable situations.

Of course, knowledge isn't the only component to great customer service. The buying experience should also be pleasant—so reminding your front line employees always to be courteous and friendly is essential. Arm them with the information they'll need to help their customers, but also remember that a pleasant personality helps a great deal—which begins with keeping the employee's own problems away from the customer.

Making a Difference

Training should be ongoing, but don't throw everything at your employees at the same time. Don't stress them out or overwhelm them with too much information at any given time. The object is to train them well, so they'll stay with you for some time, because having long-term employees saves time and money on having to train new people, and creates a feeling of stability in the minds of your customers.

As always, the ultimate goal is to build customer trust and loyalty, so that they'll continue to return for more of your products and services—which adds up to increased income! When it comes to customers, remind all your employees that as doctors, it's their job to listen to their customers' concerns and needs and then provide solutions. When that concept becomes thoroughly ingrained into everyone's thinking, your company will have made a strong start toward providing excellent customer service.

Remember: superior customer service excellence isn't hard to achieve, as long as it's approached one customer, one product, and one day at a time.

Encourage your front line employees to take time, like doctors, to let the last customer's situation go before moving on to the next customer. If the previous customer was difficult, let your people know that they have your approval to take a few minutes to walk away and collect themselves before taking on their next customer. That's better than letting the ill feelings from a previous customer spill over to their next transaction. Give your employees permission to take some time to cool off, to the point where they can approach their next customer with a genuine smile—one that lets their customers know they're prepared to be the doctor, listen to their situation, and then propose a solution that's in everyone's best interest. Keeping employee stress levels as low as possible helps everyone.

Always insist on honesty and accountability from your salespeople, and you'll minimize your customer service problems later on. If a customer isn't knowledgeable about a product, have your people go out of their way to explain all facets of the product and how it will help solve the customer's concerns Your customers will be grateful, and they'll keep returning for the same great service they experienced.

In the end, it doesn't matter what product or serviced you're selling—the concept of superior customer service is the same. Genuinely listen to your customers, like a doctor would, never looking down on them for not knowing as much as you do. In fact, that's the whole point: they initially came to your company precisely because they didn't know how to solve their needs or concerns, and they're looking to you for expert advice.

If you think like a doctor, you'll find a way to fix their problem.

Statistics show that the companies that routinely show up on the list of the top ten most profitable businesses are also on the list of best companies to work for. What that implies is that when companies loosen the purse strings and begin to take care of their employees, making them feel like valuable members of a team, their employees then take better care of their customers. That superior customer service then translates to repeat business and positive word of mouth advertising, which in turn translates to increased profits. It's a snowball effect, and it benefits everyone concerned.

So remember, spending a little more time and money toward training your employees to think like doctors isn't really an expenditure. It's actually an investment in your company's long-term health and profitability.

Like doctors, everyone in your organization should constantly be striving for 100% customer satisfaction, and that begins by instilling this mantra in every employee's mind: "You're the doctor, so fix the problem."

11

Getting Employees to Care about Your Company and Customers

As always, we'll begin by scrubbing up, in preparation for new information that will help you move toward your goal of providing superior customer service within your organization. Relax, take a few deep breaths, open your mind, and then let's move on to our discussion of how to encourage your employees to begin thinking like doctors.

Are Your Employees at the Top of Their Game?

Let's begin by thinking about the impression you get when you initially walk into a business establishment. What do you notice first? If you're like me, it's the décor that first catches my eye. Then I notice whether the product I'm looking for is easy to locate. If it's not, my next impression is of how easy it is to find a salesperson to assist me I don't want to have to search all over the store for a clerk, and when I find one, I want that person to greet me in a friendly, courteous manner. I'm looking for a smile and an expression that gives me the feeling that the salesperson is glad I came in and is eager to help solve whatever issues I may be encountering.

If you've gone into a store and couldn't find the merchandise you're looking for, and then also couldn't locate a salesperson to help you, you know what a negative impression that created. You felt as if you were being treated like just another person to be dealt with, rather than as a special guest in the store, one deserving of special treatment. It certainly wasn't acceptable customer service, and that negative impression will linger in your mind every time you think about that store from that day on.

It's sad to say, but there are many companies that give you such a cold, uncaring feeling when you first walk in their place of business. That happens because there's nothing in the job for the employees except a paycheck, so they have no incentive to make your visit as a customer special—and they're certainly not thinking like doctors! This is especially true with department stores, except for those few select companies that really have the concept of superior customer service down pat.

Our focus in this chapter is on how you can create a caring, responsible attitude among your employees—one that will permeate your entire organization and will easily be felt by every customer who enters your business establishment. It all begins with getting your employees to genuinely care about your company and customers!

Companies that exhibit a caring attitude toward their employees and customers consistently outperform the industry average, regardless of which industry they may be in. These are companies that really have a handle of how to get their employees to care for their customers and company, and they're the ones that are consistently on top, whether economic times are good or bad.

When you shop at these stores, you instantly notice the positive, helpful attitude of the employees. They're friendly and seem genuinely happy to be there They also make it clear that they're happy to see you, and they're eager to find out how they can help. They make you feel good from the moment you walk in the door—and that's the type of attitude you want to instill in every one of your employees.

Good Investment Tips

To achieve those results, here are some suggestions, although they may be difficult to accept at first. But remember, you're making an investment, meant to pay off over the long haul, and not just for the short term. So keep your mind open, like the doctor you are, remembering that just because the information that you're about to read may be new and different to you, that doesn't mean it's not relevant and important to your company's long-term success. After all, even the medical field is constantly changing as new information comes to light. If that weren't the case, doctors would still be bleeding people for a wide-ranging number of common ailments. Times change, and treatments change as well, so no matter how difficult you may find what we're about to discuss, store it away on your mind's shelf for future reference. Trust me—eventually, it will all come in handy.

One of the key factors to getting your employees to care for your company and your customers is money! In fact, making more money is one of the most important considerations for a great many people in the workforce today. When people begin looking for employment, they may hear good things about your company, but if your pay scale isn't at least as good—and better is preferable—to the industry average, you won't get the chance to see those people's applications. The best, brightest, and most capable employees will be looking for companies that will show them respect—and part of that respect will be shown in the attractiveness of a company's pay package.

People are always looking to better themselves, and if you want to attract quality employees, you must offer a strong incentive for them to come and work for you, rather than for your competition. Of course, I'm not suggesting that you simply throw your money away—but make no mistake: attracting quality employees isn't an expense, it's an investment! After all, no team can expect to win without signing up quality players, and quality players cost money.

It's like investing in the stock market. Let's say you got a tip from a reliable source, a good friend, about a company that you'd never heard of. Their stock was selling for $5.00 a share, but your friend told you that the company was about to come out with a new product that would revolutionize their industry, and once that happened, that company's share prices would probably go up to $100.00. The question is: would you buy that stock, based solely on its potential and the recommendation of a trusted source of information?

The same principle applies when it comes to hiring quality employees and nurturing your present employees. If their credentials and references are impeccable, and if you get a positive feeling from their personality and their resume, it's your responsibility as head of your organization to do everything you can to make those people a part of your team—and once you've accomplished that, you need to help them succeed.

It takes a combination of hard-nosed examination of every prospective employee's resume and an intuitive assessment of that person's latent potential if you're going to build a winning business team. But recognizing potential isn't an exact science, as all professional sports teams can attest. Every year, there's a draft, in which teams pick the individuals they believe will help better their situation in their respective league. But every year, there are some highly-touted players who don't help their team nearly as much as the owners hoped. On the other hand, there are often players who were drafted in one of the later rounds who go on to become superstars.

It's your job to try to assemble the best team possible, and then to do your best to give each employee the opportunity to rise to their greatest potential So when you contemplate hiring new people, think in terms of their potential, always looking for that intangible spark that can offer hints as to their ability to rise to the top of your organization. Then, once you've hired that person, give them the tools and the encouragement to begin making that climb. Invest in employees who will be happy to make sure that your customers are getting the most out of each visit to your place of business and then leaving totally satisfied and happy—your entire team will benefit as a result.

Quality Employees

Since you'll be paying better wages, you should begin attracting above-average applicants for your team. Invest in those people—it's an investment in your entire company. Let every employee in your organization know that you've taken a chance on them because you truly believe that they have the ability to treat your customers well and to treat the company as if it was their own. Let them know that you're investing in their future, believing that they'll, in turn, invest in the company's future—and that you'll be holding them accountable for all of their actions at all times.

Employees love it when that kind of trust is placed in them. It shows respect, and gives them a sense of pride and responsibility for the survival and growth of their company. In truth, the investment you'll be making in dollars will be secondary to the importance of the investment you'll be making in making every employee feel as if they're a valuable member of your team. After all, there are psychic benefits to any job that go beyond a simple paycheck. Knowing that they're respected and valued, and being reminded of that fact every day through in the quality of their workplace is extremely valuable to your employees, even though it doesn't have to cost a great deal of extra money to accomplish.

The payoff for all this is well worth the investment. The morale of your workplace will be good, productivity will increase, and employee turnover will be reduced, thereby saving on training costs. All that positive energy will be translated into a friendly staff, which will then pass those good vibes on to your customers It's the classic win-win situation, and everyone benefits.

Starting your employees out at a pay scale that's only slightly higher than the competition and then offering slightly higher increases than your competitors each year will attract quality people and keep them from shopping around for a better position somewhere else as time goes by. Never forget, what we're talking about is an investment: you put out a certain amount now in order to receive a significantly increased benefit over time.

Great Methods to Consider

So far, we've talked about investing in employee wages, but many employees don't work for a strict hourly wage—they make their living either through commissions or through a combination of an hourly wage and commissions. If you have positions in your organization that pay according to either one of those scenarios, you'll want to think out your payment schedules very carefully—always thinking in terms of win-win, and in terms of attracting and keeping a successful team together.

You may even want to consider adding some sort of commission-based incentives that would allow employees to be able to increase their wages through improved sales Such programs would allow your people to benefit directly from their additional efforts, which is always a formula for improving both morale and job satisfaction The happier your employees are, the more they'll pass on those good feelings to your customers, which will bring in repeat business and increase positive word of mouth advertising. Be creative. Think about ways you can offer incentives to your employees for increased productivity. Every business is different, of course, but there are always avenues that can be explored, regardless of your company's situation.

The next big factor for increasing worker pride and loyalty is health insurance. We all know that health insurance is a great concern among the workforce today, and offering your employees a health benefit will make obtaining jobs at your company even more highly prized.

In America today, more and more families are uninsured, and have no health coverage to protect them, in the event of an unexpected catastrophe. Therefore, unless something changes, offering a health plan to your employees will continue to be an important benefit and will help keep your people from moving on to your competition or risking the loss of that plan while they search for a new job.

Creating a Successful Customer Service Project

Paying your people well, showing them respect and holding them accountable, and offering a health plan will go a long way toward building the strong, talented team you're looking for. You'll be surrounded with a loyal staff who will love working for your organization and won't be constantly looking to find greener pastures—and that stability will inspire customer confidence, as well.

It's hard to understate the importance of taking care of your employees—taking care of your people is the best way to take care of your overall business. It builds loyalty and pride, and encourages maximum effort and accountability. Again, it's an investment in your company's future—one that will pay off handsomely in the long run.

When you hold staff meetings, you can always give your people the usual pep talks, but make sure to set aside time for employee feedback, as well. Let employees discuss their concerns, because they're on the front lines and will often have insights you won't be aware of. Don't take their concerns personally. If you really do consider them part of your team, you must also believe that your employees' concerns are being voiced in the best interest of the entire team. Don't make your employees come in on their days off, and once the meeting is in progress, make sure that everyone gets a chance to share their input. Meetings should be times for speaking out and trying to improve the team's chance of winning.

You might think of meetings as the equivalent of halftimes at a sporting event. The team huddles up, the head coach talks for awhile, and then players offer the insights they've gained while toiling in the trenches. Then the coaches make adjustments, based on the information their players have shared. At the end of the meeting, everyone heads back to the game, armed with new strategies for success and confident of victory.

You can also use mystery shoppers to gain insights into employee attitudes and effectiveness, as well. Mystery shopper feedback can be worthwhile in assessing the overall health of your operation on the front lines, allowing you to make adjustments that you might otherwise never have known needed to be made. Mystery shoppers can verify that all of your customers are being treated exactly the way that you want them to be treated—through superior customer service!

As is the case with a team owner, hoping to find a superstar among the lower draft picks, you'll want to keep an eye out for employees in your organization who are showing great potential when taking care of your customers. Create award programs that will allow you to recognize excellence among your employees and to provide increased incentive for raising the customer service bar for your entire organization. Make sure to reward your star performers in some real, tangible way, as well as recognition. It doesn't have to be a huge monetary reward, but the award needs to be significant enough to make it a prize worth shooting for by every employee.

Offering an above-average wage, treating each employee with respect, offering a health package, being open to suggestions, and rewarding superior performance will go a long way toward helping your employees care about your company and its customers It's a long-term investment, but as you build a strong, loyal team, your organization's profits will increase— along with those psychic benefits that can't be measured on a typical graph.

Let every employee know that you expect them to be totally accountable for their own actions, and teach them to think and act like doctors. And as we've said many times before, keep repeating your slogan until it becomes ingrained in every employee's psyche: "You're the doctor, so fix the problem!"

12

Times are Changing: Importance of Communication

Well, we're coming to the end of our discussion, but we still have a couple more things to consider, so let's scrub up before we take a look at how things are changing in the United States with regard to customer service. Take a few moments to relax your thoughts, take a couple deep breaths, and open your mind to the information that's about to come. Let everything else go, and begin to look forward to expanding your horizons even further. Then, when you're ready, we'll move on.

Keeping Abreast of Changing Times

In this chapter, we'll be talking about how much things have changed in the U.S. and how important it is that businesses continue to change if they're going to keep up with the rest of the economy and the competition within their particular industries. The Internet has affected the way business is done today, but it's only one aspect of the incredible changes that have taken place within the realm of business communication. American companies are getting larger, to the point that two or three giant corporations generally dominate their respective industries, which leaves fewer and fewer choices where consumers can do their everyday shopping. However, those giant companies have gotten huge in large part because they know how to keep their customers happy. Customers won't feel the need to visit their competitors, because those large companies have made shopping a satisfying experience. In other words, they've gotten the art of superior customer service down to an exact science.

That type of success is a testament to what can happen when companies focus their efforts on making their customers happy—and that type of customer service is exactly what you'll want to emulate in your own organization if you want to succeed. Its how every company should conduct its business, regardless of what industry they happen to be engaged in. Superior customer service is always desirable in every business situation, without exception. It may take some time to implement great customer service in your organization, but the results will definitely be worth the effort.

However, staying on top means changing with the times, and if those giant companies fail to do that, it creates opportunities for their smaller competitors. For example, there are millions of people from different parts of the world now living in the United States, more than at any other time in our nation's history. This means that many business adjustments need to be made, but it also gives smaller companies an advantage, because they're generally able to implement changes more quickly than the big corporations, which are saddled by ponderous bureaucracies.

Many companies aren't taking the steps necessary to adjust to a large diversity of clientele, especially in their hiring practices. In my own experience, I've often seen customers walk into a place of business to do their shopping, but because they didn't speak English, they were left to work their way through the store without any assistance from salespeople at all.

At other times, I've seen such people struggle to communicate with a salesperson who didn't understand their language, which can often be an even bigger disaster. The poor customer is trying to convey their needs, but the salesperson is unable to understand what they're saying, and the customer can't comprehend the English being used by the salesperson—so the frustration level increases of both sides of the transaction.

That's one situation that American businesses need to address. Have you ever traveled to a foreign country and tried to ask directions from someone who speaks no English? I have, and it gave me a much deeper appreciation for the way customers from other parts of the world must feel when only they're trying to get their shopping done—with or without a salesperson's assistance.

But this is an area in which you can gain a competitive advantage, if you're willing to expand your horizons. You can pull ahead of your competitors by offering services for those customers who speak little or no English. By doing so, you'll find those customers turning to your company for their daily shopping, and that's a very large potential market, one that could significantly improve your bottom line!

Your Company Will Take Off

One way of working with such a diverse group of customers is to hire employees who can speak the same langue as the customer base you're hoping to begin bringing into your place of business. But you must be selective when hiring employees for this type of project, making sure that each new employee processes excellent commutation skills. Once you've hired employees with diverse background, it's important to set up a system by which those employees can be called upon at any time of the day to assist customers who may be having trouble communicating their needs to another salesperson. The position doesn't need to be full-time, but the communication person's hours should correspond with the peak hours for needing their translation services, whatever those hours may be for your particular organization.

You could further enhance feelings of good will by posting your signs in a combination of the most common languages throughout your place of business. These multilingual signs can be used to point the way to restrooms, customer service, and any other areas that generate high traffic during the day.

That's the type of progressive thinking that can give your organization an edge over your competition. It's also called moving along with changing times—both for your customers and employees. It's also called providing superior customer service.

Whether they're multilingual or simply English-speaking, employees with good communication skills are a must in any type of business today. Any time communication breaks down, it's like throwing money out of the window, and no company can afford to do that. So no matter which position you're filling in your organization, be very selective in the hiring process.

Just think about the last time you had to deal with a salesperson without good communication skills. It soured the entire buying process, and may have even led to some misunderstanding about the product, its warranty, or some other important piece of information. No one is a stranger to this sort of situation, because it happens all the time. Anyone who has ever had to shop for anything has experienced it at some point, but it doesn't have to be that way, and if you continually hire people with good communication skills, it won't happen to your customers.

Emphasizing good communication goes hand in hand with teaching your employees to think like doctors. Doctors ask lots of questions of their patients, and then they listen to the answers before asking another question. They're not trying to sell a patient on one remedy or another as soon as they walk into the examining room. They listen to the patient's problems, and then find a suitable solution.

In every situation, every day, constantly remind your employees, "You're the doctor, so fix the problem!"

Going just a little extra distance makes a huge difference, and puts you ahead of the vast majority of your competitors, who are simply trying to sell merchandise or services, rather than genuinely trying to fix their customer's problems But once you've introduced your customers to great customer service, they'll never forget that experience and will keep returning for the same great treatment—again and again.

You're Closer than Ever Before!

The reason superior customer service is so important is, unfortunately, because people seldom are able to find it anymore. There are many reasons for skimping on customer service, of course. For instance, many companies are looking to save money by cutting back on labor costs. But as we've all experienced, there's nothing more frustrating than to have to look all over a store for someone to assist you. So cutting back on help may save labor cost, but it has a genuine negative effect on your customer's impression of your business, and that will ultimately reflect on your bottom line.

As we've shown throughout this book, creating a great customer service program in your company isn't all that expensive to implement, and will pay huge dividends over time. When your customers have positive experiences at your place of business, they'll return—and they'll bring their friends and family with them. Positivity breeds more positivity and providing great service is the best way to jumpstart your profits.

If you still have doubts, let's compare two nearly identical department stores, both selling essentially the same products, but one of those stores sells those products for 10-20% less than the other. Many customers will shop at the store with the discounted prices, based strictly on the price savings.

But let's say that the other store has a friendly feel when you first walk in. The employees seem happy to be there, and seem delighted to see you. They greet you in a friendly fashion, maybe even calling you by your name, and if you're a non-English-speaking person, perhaps they greet you in your native language, as well. They ask how you're doing, and seem genuinely interested in doing their best to assist you with whatever brought you into their store.

Now let's take the comparison a step farther. Let's say that you're looking for a piece of merchandise that's out of stock, but you really need as soon as possible. In the first store, you're simply told, without using the exact words that you're out of luck, and to try back later.

But at the second store, a salesperson checks to see when they'll have the item back in stock, and if that's not acceptable, they either help you find a different solution to your problem or they grab a phone book and help locate your particular product on the spot. If the competitor's store happens to be some distance away, they might even offer to order it and have it shipped to you.

Truthfully, now—which store would you be more loyal to in the long run? Would you be willing to go to the second store more often than the first one, even if their prices are slightly higher? That's right, you'd choose to return to the second store, and from my own experience of working with customers day after day, I can tell you that you wouldn't be alone in making that decision. Customers respond to excellent customer service, and they come back for more.

So always bear in mind that it's not necessary to give away your merchandise by playing the price war game. In the long run, customers are drawn to great customer service, even if they have to pay a slight premium to get it. Word of mouth gets around when you go the extra mile to help your customers live better lives—which involves thinking and acting like a doctor, and fixing your customer's problems.

When someone moves to a new town, one of the first things on their list of things to do is to find a good doctor. They'll ask their friends and family members, and will visit the doctor who has the strongest reputation for great results. Think about it. When you find an excellent doctor, don't you tell your friends?

The same is true for businesses that have great reputations for customer service People tell other people, and business increases. It's a simple formula I've seen it happen time after time, and I know it works. So hire good communicators, give them to the proper training, hold them accountable at all times, make them feel like valuable members of your team, and they'll respond by taking excellent care of your customers.

Staying Ahead of the High-Tech World

Now that we've covered communication in respect to our face-to-face customers, let's look at its importance to your organization's presence on the Internet and on the phone. Internet customer service can be a delicate subject, because it's easy to forget the value of each customer after receiving an instantaneous payment through an Internet transaction.

It's important to create a department dedicated solely to dealing with your company's Internet customers. The staff should be low-key, patient, and must possess a strong ability to identify and communicate with your customers, whether it's via email, telephone, or letter. The Internet allows your company to create a worldwide presence that was never possible to such a great degree before. Your customer may be in Paris, Illinois or Paris, France, but your staff needs to make either customer feel important, regardless of where they happen to live. There should be no difference between the excellence of service on the Internet or in person.

Internet customer service agents must have great people skills, as well as being equally well versed in the high tech Internet sales process. They must be able to multi-task, and must understand every aspect of the Internet sales process. After all, just one phone call will generally cover the shipping functions—warehouse locations, modes of delivery, tracking, scheduling of packing, availability of goods, and return/exchange policies. It will usually also involve payment functions (verifying payment methods and proper application of monies received), goods/services offered (item descriptions and numbers), and many other customer service issues.

Through it all, the salesperson must maintain a helpful, caring attitude at all times, always making the customer glad they got in touch with your company in the first place. The Internet contains its own brand of challenges, so choose your Internet department staff carefully, just as you do with every other department in your organization—always keeping superior customer service foremost in your mind.

Equip your customer service agents with excellent training and software support, so they can offer your customers solutions to their problems in a timely manner, whether they're dealing with Internet clients or talking to customers on the phone If your 800# puts customers on hold for 15 minutes, even after forcing them to enter countless amounts of information after ten prompts before they could speak to a live human being, your company's reputation for being caring and responsible is going to suffer. It will also add fuel to the fire of that person who called your customer service department with a problem in the first place, because it will only add to their frustration.

Whenever possible, it's important to equip your customer service agents with the ability to handle all of your customer challenges during the course of only one phone call. This can't be stressed enough. Shifting people from one person to another only adds to their frustration level, and also increases the possibility of having them be cut off, which is one of the most frustrating things that can happen to a person who is already upset. So handle every caller with just one phone call whenever possible.

There's nothing that tells customers they're not important to a company like being on hold, having to answer a dozen useless prompts from a computer, and then getting cut off, which forces them to go through the entire process again. We've all been there, and know exactly how powerless and frustrated we feel while we're being subjected to that whole process—and make no mistake: the effect on your bottom line can be just as devastating as poor face-to-face contact with your customers.

So always put some of your best communicators in your Internet and phone departments, because they need to have the skills to turn unhappy customers into repeat customers—through the use of the great customer service tools you've provided them Make sure they genuinely listen to customer concerns, and then work hard to resolve those issues. They may never meet any of your company's customers face to face, but they still need to think like doctors, nonetheless.

As team players, they're responsible to pick up the ball if a teammate has dropped it, and to run with it. They need to repair any damage that a problem has caused the customer, to offer their apologies, and then to assure that customer that it won't happen again.

Just remind your people: communication involves twice as much listening as talking. That's one reason we have two ears and only one mouth. Regardless of which department your people work in, communication is of the utmost importance. By communicating well, your employees are also representing your company well.

Let every employee know that developing good communication skills is a huge part of learning to think and act like a doctor. They need to ask lots of pertinent questions, listen carefully to the answers, and once the client has given them all the information they believe is relevant, then—and only then— should the employee offer a solution.

But it all begins with good basic communication, whether it's in English or some other language. Doctors know that instinctively, and it's a way of thinking you need to instill in every employee in your organization, from top to bottom.

So whenever one of your people comes to you for advice, your first words to them should always be, "You're the doctor, so fix the problem!"

13

Think Before You Act

We're almost to the end of the book, so you should be well familiar with what comes first in the process. It will be the last time we'll be scrubbing up together, but I hope you'll continue to use the process in your daily life. It will help you remain centered and ready for each new challenge and situation that may arise. Thinking like the doctor you are, will not only change your life, but also the lives of everyone with whom you come into contact.

So let's go ahead and scrub up, and then we'll get on with the summary of what we've covered in this book. Take the time to allow your mind to become clear and your thoughts to become still. Take a few deep breaths, and then you'll be ready to address whatever concerns you encounter with your next customer, employee, or task. Whatever it may be, you'll be focused and ready to tackle it with a clear mind and fresh perspective.

Responding Clearly and Thoughtfully

As we've talked about in the preceding chapters, doctors never move forward to their next patient without taking the time to mentally finish with their previous patient They never let what happened previously affect what they're about to encounter next. They release all previous information and any attendant emotions, and then move on to the next patient—in the best interest for everyone concerned.

When you're in the right frame of mind, let's move on to our final look at how you can create great customer service within your organization. First, let's begin by asking yourself if you really take the time needed to genuinely understand the concerns of your customers and employees before moving forward, each and every time? Or do you jump into whatever issue is before you at the moment, not really understanding the situation fully and just hoping for the best?

Regardless of what the issue or project you may have at hand, the best results are always obtained from a well designed and carefully implemented plan. Even if you should fall short of your ultimate goal, in most cases, you won't be far off the mark, because you've given the situation a considerable amount of thought and have tried to consider every possibility before you began.

On the other hand, if you simply set out with no plan, you'll normally fall short of your intended objective, and whatever repairs may be necessary as a result will be difficult to implement because you won't have any definite steps you can retrace. That's one of the biggest reasons for having a well conceived plan—it allows you to backtrack and regroup when you run into an unforeseen obstacle. You can take a couple steps back before you make your next move, allowing you to carefully consider what actions will best address whatever difficulties you've encountered. Then, as you move forward, make sure to share everything you've learned along the way, and pass it on to your customers and employees.

It's also important for you to keep your emotions in check, and not to lash out at those around you when things aren't going exactly according to plan How many times in your life has someone offended you by their words or actions, and then you made the situation worse by responding impulsively, only to regret your reaction later? As human beings, we instinctively try to protect ourselves from perceived threats of harm or danger. We often say or do things that we'd take back if we had the chance, but in business, there are many times when we won't be given a second chance by our customers. So always guard against an off-hand remark or reaction that you'll later regret.

It's a universal situation—one that everyone experiences from time to time But armed with this warning, you can minimize the risk and associated cost, in terms of lost revenue, that can be incurred when you act before thinking. Remember, great customer service requires constant awareness of the situation and attention to detail. Think like the doctor you are, and always keep your thoughts focused on how to fix the problem.

When you're considering how to improve the quality, as well as the quantity of your business, the theme we've emphasized in the previous chapters continues to be relevant. That is, when you're in the customer service business (which all businesses are), you're always acting in a subservient role, constantly striving to satisfy your customer's wants and needs. If you're doing it right, that's your only reason for being in business, and your method of serving your customers is the most important factor in determining their level of satisfaction—which, in turn, will ultimately determine the success of your business.

If you want to achieve better customer service results, take yourself out of the picture and focus solely on making your customers happy. If you continue to do that, day after day, everyone wins. Your customers will be pleased with your products and services and they'll be anxious the share their excitement with their network of family and friends. They'll also return as customers themselves, again and again, as long as your commitment to superior customer service remains in tact.

However, the opposite holds true when your customers walk away from a transaction dissatisfied They'll tell everyone who will listen about their negative experience, and your business will suffer, to the point of failing, if the unsatisfactory customer service situation isn't resolved.

Customer service isn't difficult to implement, and is crucial to your business success. It just requires taking yourself out of the picture and turning your sole focus toward pleasing someone else and meeting their needs, even during those times when you might feel as if you're not meeting your own.

It's All Very Clear—Now Move Forward

Regardless of what may be happening in your life, your focus must always be on your customers No matter how tough your day has been, you can't allow that to taint your interactions with your customers.

Always bear our catch phrase in mind: "You're the doctor, so fix the problem."

Your customers walk into your place of business seeking advice and a solution to whatever concerns they're facing. Like the doctor you are, you can't show your personal problems to your customers. You must make each customer confident that your only goal is to help them solve their problems, as quickly and efficiently as possible. Remember: they're the customer and you're the advisor, whose sole purpose in each transaction is to make their lives better through your sincere efforts.

Never engage in a power struggle with your customer by arguing back and forth. It's always counterproductive. Regardless of how difficult the customer may become, you must remain calm, always remembering that they initially sought you out for help, which was an act of respect on their part for you and your organization. In every customer interaction, it's your job to make them glad they turned to you for a solution to their concerns, issues, and needs.

Even if your customer remains irate and belligerent, staying calm is still your best tactic for helping that person. In the worst case scenario, the customer will walk away, but will probably regret their actions later. They may even seek you out again for future business, once cooler heads have prevailed. In the best case scenario, your calm attitude will allow the customer to vent their frustration and then, once they've calmed down, you can get on with the business of finding a solution to their concerns that had frustrated them so much in the beginning. In the end, that's all your customers really want, anyway—answers to their needs. Provide them, and your success is assured.

So don't take customer affronts personally. They're not mad at you—they're just mad. Your best strategy is to remain calm until the customer is finished with their venting process, and then to assure them that you're committed to helping find a solution to their situation. It will let your customers know they're dealing with a caring individual who sees them as more than just a number on a spreadsheet—a person who is obviously dedicated to alleviating their stress and helping them move on with their lives.

Once you've achieved this understanding, you'll both win. Meeting another person's needs allows you to gain a great deal in return, and that's the true art of providing superior customer service. It simply requires the ability to relate to and interact with various types of people who are encountering difficulties that have caused them to seek out your professional help and advice That's a perfect description of what doctors do, wouldn't you agree?

My Personal Experience

I experienced an example of how not to provide customer service in my own life some time ago. One of my colleagues was observing a training class being facilitated by someone else. The facilitator opened the topic for discussion, and then lost control of the audience. In an effort to assist the facilitator in regaining control of the class, my colleague jumped in and tried to redirect the conversation. However, it was too late at that point, because by that time, two of the class members were already engaged in a rather serious confrontation.

My colleague's efforts to redirect the class discussion had failed because she herself had become noticeably frustrated. Then, unable to control her own frustration, she angrily singled out one of the class members by name and instructed that person to be quiet. Although it was a class of adults, my colleague immediately felt the knot in her stomach as she realized that she'd singled out one of the class members in the same manner that an elementary school teacher would have done when trying to silence the class clown.

When it was time for the class to take a break, the class member who'd been singled out told the others that she'd been insulted by my colleague's treatment, and was leaving as a result. That created a negative vibe for the rest of the class members, and my colleague had to do a lot of damage control work when the class resumed, addressing the issue with the remaining class members and making sure that they regained their positive feelings about the organization and the meeting they were attending. My colleague also had to call the slighted individual into her office the next day and apologize, but the damage had been done, and the interaction between them was never quite the same from that day on.

So always think before you act, and when it comes to your customers, keep your own feelings under control. Focus on your customer's needs, and never let your personal feelings get in the way of providing the type of service every customer wants—and deserves.

Put it Into Action Every Day

At the end of the every workday, you should honestly be able to say to yourself, "I gave it my best."

It's important to understand that what you have to offer is one of the greatest gifts in the world—the ability to identify a customer's needs and then match those needs with a product and service that will perfectly fill them In the process, you'll be encouraging your customers to identify with your organization, which means you'll be the first company they'll think of when facing their next problem in your area of expertise. Maintain your honesty, trust, and caring attitude, and combine those attributes with knowledge and true accountability, and your business will succeed—period.

Here's something else to consider. Over the course of my long customer service career, I've run across a number of examples of long-time employees who began to think that the company they worked for belonged to them. Of course, you want your employees to feel as if they're a valuable member of your team, but when they begin to react before thinking in ways that are inconsistent with company policy, that can negatively affect your customers' perception of the overall organization. If employees are making customers upset or uncomfortable, those customers may leave and never return. So it's vital to let your people know company policies, and then reinforce the fact that you're doing them the courtesy of holding them responsible for making sure those policies are being carried out at all times. If all of your employees are truly thinking like doctors and members of a skilled team of professionals, that should never be a problem.

As we mentioned earlier, that's one reason mystery shoppers can be effective in making sure everyone, especially those on the front lines, is acting responsibly and being fully accountable for their actions at all times—especially when it comes to dealing with customers. You can't watch every employee's interactions with customers at all times, so mystery shoppers can be a valuable resource for maintaining your organization's customer service at a consistently high level.

Total accountability, by every employee in your business, is the most important factor in creating the kind of excellent customer service that will bring customers flocking to your doors. That means thinking like doctors and then taking care of the customer, each time, every time—without fail.

Whenever your business seems to start seeing less traffic or more complaints, you can be assured that there's been a lapse in your employees' level of the accountability, which will always have an adverse effect on your company's customer service. If you begin to see a serious dip in business traffic, you'll need to take steps immediately to reemphasize your company's customer service policies, because a significant decrease in business can nearly always be traced to how a company is taking care of its customers. If everyone doesn't think like a doctor, your sales will fall, your clientele will decrease, and your bottom line will suffer.

It's that simple—yet I can't stress that point strongly enough, or often enough!

So always be on the lookout for employees who don't seem to care about your company and their role within it. Those employees are far more likely to say or do something before they think the situation through, which will immediately have a negative impact on your customers.

If your employees are having trouble grasping the concept of thinking like doctors, offer them this scenario. Have them think back to the last time they visited a doctor themselves. When they got to the examination room and the doctor came in, what was the first thing the doctor did? Generally, the doctor entered the room, looking at the patient's chart, and immediately showed sympathy for the fact that the patient wasn't feeling well. Then, the doctor began asking questions about the nature of the symptoms, gathering information about how the patient felt, if there was a history of such a complaint, where it hurt, how long it had been going on, and many others. The patient was then reassured that their doctor was truly interested in finding a solution to whatever was ailing them.

What the doctor did not do was argue with the patient, give them a stern lecture, or cut them off in the middle of a sentence to add something of their own, whether it was helpful or not. The focus was always squarely on the patient, and there was never any doubt that the doctor was there exclusively to help solve the problem.

That's the kind of thinking you must instill in every employee, from top to bottom of your organization, and once you've done that, you're going to be amazed at the difference, both in the increased quantity of business you'll attract, and the improved quality of your company workplace Take care of every issue that arises with your customers, whether in person, by letter, by email, or by phone—without exception—is crucial to your company's success.

Constantly remind your employees, "You're the doctor, so fix the problem."

Also remind them that being held accountable for their actions is your way of showing respect and concern for your employees. You expect them to treat each customer as the most important person in the world at that particular moment, just as a doctor would Keeping that thought in mind will eliminate any possibility that employees will provide anything less than the best customer service at any given time.

Every employee is important to your business team's success. You simply can't emphasize this enough to your people. One employee who isn't giving superior customer service can hurt business in significant ways, even though they may never know about the serious negative impact they caused by not acting like a doctor during any particular transaction.

Putting the Concept into Action

Throughout this book, our mantra has been, "You're the doctor, so fix the problem."

Once everyone in your organization begins to act like doctors, your profits will increase as you change your old ways of doing business. Think like doctors, keeping your customers happy and letting them know that you're committed to taking care of their needs, issues and concerns. Do that every day and customers will continue to come back to your place of business for all of their own needs. They'll also tell their friends, family, and business acquaintances, and that best of all advertising— word of mouth—will begin gathering momentum in your favor.

It's not good enough to simply have a plan for good customer service within your company. That plan must become thoroughly ingrained in every employee's psyche, until they can't imagine treating customers any other way. Once superior customer service becomes a way of life, your people will find it impossible to give customers anything less, simply because it won't feel right to do so. Giving anything less than their absolute best will be unthinkable—and your customers will respond in ways that will amaze you.

Now is the time to take charge of your company and lead your employees in a new direction, one that will instantly begin to affect your bottom line, because your customers will see the difference, and your employees will feel a new sense of empowerment and conviction. Thinking like doctors is the best example of how to give great customer service. Instill those types of thought patterns in your employees, and your company will be well on its way to rising above the competition.

Ask yourself this question: how often have you gone into a doctor's office and come out with anything other than at least a 90% feeling of satisfaction? Keep in mind that the world isn't a perfect place, so even though there may have been times when your experience may have been less than you might have hoped, you probably still came away from your visit believing that the doctor made a genuine, heartfelt effort to help solve your problem. What's more, you will probably return to that same doctor the next time you experience a health issue.

Even when they're thinking and acting like doctors, your employees may not always be able to solve every problem exactly to the customer's satisfaction, but that should always be their goal, and you must give them the power to do so. That's what doctors do—they take whatever actions will be necessary to solve the problem. And if it requires more tests or bringing in a specialist, than that's what they will do. The same is true for you and the way your company treats its customers. You're always striving for 100% satisfaction, even though it's not always possible. Even so, that should never stop you from constantly trying to reach that goal.

Just as a doctor's business is called a "practice," your company should always be practicing how to provide your customers with outstanding customer service. Practice improving your service to each and every customer, and you'll get better and better at it, until 90% of your customers will walk away from their transactions with your place of business, satisfied and happy with the service they received.

Of course, that type of commitment requires total accountability from everyone in your organization, but once your people begin thinking like doctors, you'll find that it's easily achievable. As long as every employee believes they have the ability to solve every problem their customers may face, your company will continue to expand its horizons, your company will grow, your profits will increase, and your employees will have a much more enjoyable work experience every day. What could be better than that?

Conclusion

So as we draw this book to a close, let's recap the key points we've discussed. No matter what field you're in, you can make your business better, even if it's already a good company, by getting your employees to focus on providing excellent customer service. However, you are the one who must begin the process— by taking better care of your employees, so they'll pass that care and concern on to your customers.

Get rid of your power trip, and get involved with your customers and employees. Find out what's going on within your company, at the grassroots level. Talk to as many customers and employees as possible and show a genuine concern for their concerns and insights. They'll enjoy your presence, and will begin to feel as if you really care about them. Then, as the work environment improves, morale will improve, which will translate to a more positive employee attitude with your customers.

In order to give your people an example for how to take the best care of your customers, encourage every employee to begin thinking like a doctor. Always emphasize the need for total accountability, and let your employees know that as long as they're making a genuine effort to satisfy your customers, you'll back them all the way.

Always remind your employees that great customer service is achieved exactly like a doctor achieves a successful medical practice: one customer at a time. But don't forget—that also applies to the person at the top, as well! No matter how busy your day may be or how many issues you have waiting on your desk, give your full attention to one issue, one customer, or one of your employees at a time, ensuring that everyone will be satisfied with the result.

As with most enterprises, the simplest way is generally the best, so strive to keep your customer service program simple. When setting up the program, don't expect everything to happen all at once. Keep stress levels as low as possible, and the rest will fall into place, given time and total accountability.

The simplest kind of customer service motto?

"Do whatever it takes to solve the problem."

Remind your people to always think before they act. Never do anything on an impulse. Always think issues through before responding. It will save time, frustration, and expense in the long run. There's no reason to argue with customers, and again, if your employees are constantly thinking and acting like doctors, that should never be the case.

Well, there you have them—all of the key factors that will take your company to the next level of customer service—a company that will be head and shoulders above your competition. With proper training and regular practice, your employees will begin to find themselves thinking like the doctors they truly are, concentrating their efforts on listening to customer needs, and then diligently seeking a solution As a result, your customers will be more satisfied, your company's business will increase, and your bottom line will begin to show almost immediate improvement. When you add in all the key factors we've discussed, it will be a much more pleasant place to spend a day, it all adds up to a win-win situation for everyone involved—especially the customer.

But it all begins with one simple, but profound, phrase: "You're the doctor, so fix the problem!"

Many blessings and much success.

www.ingramcontent.com/pod-product-compliance
Lightning Source LLC
Chambersburg PA
CBHW032002190326
41520CB00007B/331